Have Confidence

to

Minister

to

Others

Katherine Hilditch

'Having Confidence to Minister to Others'
By Katherine Hilditch

Copyright © 2016 Katherine Hilditch
All rights reserved.

ISBN-13: 978-1533354525

ISBN-10: 1533354529

Having Confidence to Minister to Others

Contents

Preface

This book has grown out of a ministry manual which I wrote over a number of years. It all started in 1992 when I developed M.E. In 1996 my husband and I went to a healing conference where I received miraculous healing of two debilitating aspects of the condition. I do, however, still have some symptoms. We also came home from that conference really on fire for God. As a result of this, the elders of the church we belonged to at that time asked us if we would set up a church ministry team.

We began with guidelines printed on one side of an A4 piece of paper. I did the team training and over the 17 years we led the team, I developed a manual half an inch thick. It grew as I went to further conferences, received more miracles, read and listened to sound teaching, and also through my own Bible study and God's personal revelation, and by seeing God at work as we ministered to others.

All the teaching in this book can be found in that manual, but here I am presenting it with the specific aspect of gaining confidence to minister to others. The original manual is called 'In the Name of Jesus' and can be bought online as a paperback or as an eBook. Details are on my website – www.understandingchristianity.co.uk

Katherine Hilditch

Introduction

First of all, I need to explain what I mean by 'ministry'. I am not talking about someone being called into the ministry to be a pastor or minister or vicar or priest. I am talking about coming alongside someone in need, and bringing God into their situation. You might call it praying for someone. But ministry is not the same as intercessory prayer, although it will often include it. In intercessory prayer, we ask God to work in a person's life in the future and we can pray for them whether they are with us or not. In ministry we invite, allow and expect God to work directly in the person at that moment in time. We also use the authority and power Jesus has given all Christians to defeat the strategies of Satan, including sickness, in the name of Jesus. People may ask for prayer, but what they often need is ministry. Ministry can only usually take place when the person is present.

I presume that you have a desire to see people set free from the things that hold them and walking into the victory Jesus has won for them, otherwise you would not really be interested in this book. You want to make a difference in people's lives.

But maybe that desire has some doubts alongside it. Do any of the following ring a bell with you? Do you pray for your friends and family, but nothing seems to change? Do you lack the confidence to lay hands on people? Do you doubt in your heart whether God really wants to heal and bless people today? Do you believe that He does, but doubt that He would want to use you?

3

I want this book to give you the confidence to go beyond praying for people to ministering to them in the authority Jesus has given you and in the power of the Holy Spirit, so you can then expect to see results.

You cannot minister confidently and effectively to someone if you do not have an understanding of who God is, what He is like, what Jesus has done and where the power comes from. And you cannot help someone else to understand it if you do not. But if you set out to minister with a foundation of understanding, you will be able to help people in many different ways. You need to ensure that the truth is rooted in you, because you can only pass on what you yourself understand and believe.

In the first three chapters of this book, I show you how you can have complete confidence in God, in Jesus and in the power God has given you. The fourth chapter is all about how you can have confidence in yourself, not because of your own abilities, but because of who you are in Jesus. The fifth chapter looks at how you can give confidence to the person you are ministering to, and the last chapter brings it all together with the theme of love which runs throughout the book. At the end there are over 100 Bible verses which you can use to build yourself up, and also give to others when you minister to them.

So many Christians base their theology on their own experience or on the experience of others instead of on the Word of God. For instance, if they see a person being prayed for and not getting healed, they believe God does not want that person healed. What you need to do before you can start to minster effectively, is to get your theology based on God's Word. Then, if you see few or no people being healed, you can say with confidence that you know the truth from God's Word that He always wants to heal, and can look for an alternative explanation.

Everything in this book is based on God's Word. If experience tells you something different, do not be tempted to discount what the Bible says – accept that you need to look at your experiences in a different way, and choose to believe what God's Word says instead.

Chapter 1

Confidence in God

To minister to others confidently, we have to have confidence in both God and Jesus. In this chapter we are going to look at having confidence in God. To have confidence in someone, we need to have an understanding of what they are like – what their character is and how they think, talk, act and react. In just the same way, to have confidence in God, we need to understand what He is like and how He thinks and acts.

GOD IS LOVE

God is love. Many people have a wrong picture of what God is like, seeing Him as a stern headmaster kind of figure. And many Christians struggle with what God is really like as well. They may know the fact that God loves them, but in their hearts they doubt if it is really true, or they know it is true but doubt if He loves them personally – they know themselves too well. But the Bible not only tells us that God loves us, but that He is love. It is the only attribute that the Bible says He 'is'. It is the very essence of His being, so it is going to motivate and direct and colour everything He thinks, does and says. And that love is directed towards us.

He said through the prophet Jeremiah –

"... I have loved you with an everlasting love. Therefore I have drawn you with loving kindness." (Jeremiah 31:3b)

Love is at the heart of everything God thinks about you. And it does not stop at loving thoughts. Real love always leads to actions. It was real love in action when God sent Jesus to earth to die on the Cross.

Greater love has no one than this, that someone lay down his life for his friends. (John 15:13)

God showed us just how much He loved us when He sacrificed His own Son for us. Through the Cross, Jesus shows us God's Father heart of love for each and every person individually. That includes you.

For God so loved the world, that he gave his one and only Son, that whoever believes in him should not perish, but have eternal life. (John 3:16)

In order to have real confidence in God, we have to believe He loves us with our mind and with our heart. We cannot trust Him otherwise. If we doubt His love for us, we will inevitably doubt all His words and actions towards us.

There are many ways we can describe God's love and none that are adequate, but we are going to look at two important ones.

The first is the fact that God's love is non-manipulative. When God made us He gave us free will. We are not pre-programmed robots or puppets on strings. This means that we can have a real relationship with Him. If you were able to force someone you loved to love you back, it would not be a satisfying relationship. It could even be called abuse. God leaves us free to love Him or reject Him. That way, when we do love Him back, it is a real love relationship which will not only bring joy to us, but also to Him.

And secondly, God's love is unconditional. His love for us does not depend on how we perform or measure up – it is total and unconditional.

God was in Christ reconciling the world to himself, not reckoning to them their trespasses. (2 Corinthians 5:19a)

To reckon something to someone means recording something against their name. God is not keeping a record of our sins. Instead, He has reckoned them to Jesus and Jesus has accepted and suffered the punishment on our behalf. Not only were our sins reckoned to Jesus on the Cross, but as a result, His righteousness is reckoned to us when we accept Him as our Lord and Saviour.

For him who knew no sin he made to be sin on our behalf; so that in him we might become the righteousness of God. (2 Corinthians 5:21)

Jesus became what we were so we could become what He is. Exchange has taken place. This is amazing personal love. We can never be good enough to earn God's love. But whatever we have done or not done, we are worth dying for. His love is totally unconditional.

God demonstrates His own love toward us, in that while we were still sinners, Christ died for us. (Romans 5:8)

Nothing you can do can make God love you more. Take a moment and think about that. However wonderful the things you do, they cannot make God love you more, because His love for you is already total and infinite. And nothing you can do can make God love you less. Think about that – even the most appalling sins cannot make God love you less, because His love for you is totally unconditional.

If you are going to minister to others effectively, you have to believe that God loves you unconditionally, and that He loves the person you are ministering to unconditionally as well. Anything less and there will always be doubt in your mind as to whether you can have complete confidence in God or not.

Important as it is to understand God's love, we need to go further and experience it as well. Paul tells us to –

> … know Christ's love which surpasses knowledge. *(Ephesians 3:19a)*

He says 'know' the experience of God's love, not just 'feel' it. We need to know the ongoing experience of a love relationship with God. God's love is not all about us enjoying the thrill of His touch. That is wonderful and we thank God for those times, but if you base your experience of God's love only on those times you are heading for a fall, because those mountain top experiences will not always be there. But if you base your experience of God's love on the truth you have learnt in His Word, that can never change, and even when times are difficult you can still know and experience His love personally.

God always initiates a love relationship with us, but we need to respond.

> *We love him, because he first loved us. (1 John 4:19)*

Because He loves us, we can trust Him and love Him back. He wants to have a perfect love relationship of Father and child with everyone, and it becomes reality when we accept Jesus as our Lord and Saviour.

Jesus made quite a few black and white statements. One of them was –

> *"The thief only comes to steal, kill, and destroy. I came that they may have life, and may have it abundantly."* *(John 10:10)*

If we are to have confidence in God we have to understand something of how He works and trust the way He acts. Jesus made this clear distinction between His work and the work of Satan. Good things come from God. Bad things come from Satan.

It is a lie of Satan that God sends bad things for a good purpose, and it can leave you feeling helpless. You cannot discern what is of God to take it on board, and what is of Satan to resist it.

Another deception is that God allows bad things to happen, therefore they must be His will. God does not make an individual decision about everything that could happen, whether to allow it or not. When I developed M.E. God did not think about whether to allow me to have it or not, and decide 'yes' He would. God grieves over the limits M.E. has put on me and the suffering and frustration I have had even more than I do. It is not His will just because it happened. It was Satan's work.

God made a single decision after the fall, not to step in and put everything right in the world, but to allow it to run on its messed-up course, because He will never deny us the free will He created us with. We have freedom of word and action and there are consequences to that. So troubles of all sorts arise, not as the active or passive will of God, but because He is faithful to Himself and the way He made us. This means that in this world there will always be room for Satan to manoeuvre, but he is stripped of his power by the Cross, unless we yield to him.

And God is at work in this world all the time in answer to prayer and in response to faith. He is at work in us changing us from glory to glory, and through us as we step out in the power of the name of Jesus.

We have His promise that He will work for good for us even in the bad things, but He does not send them –

We know that all things work together for good for those who love God, for those who are called according to his purpose. (Romans 8:28)

God is a good God. He loves you unconditionally. When bad things happen it is never God's fault. It is Satan who sends the bad things.

To minister effectively you have to get this sorted once and for all. If something bad has happened in someone's life, it is impossible to minister to them effectively if you do not know if God has caused it or not. And it is also impossible for the person to receive from God if they are blaming Him for their situation. Such a big part of ministry is assuring the person that God loves them totally and unconditionally and that he has not sent their problems, but is only willing good towards them.

GOD IS ON YOUR SIDE

To trust someone and have confidence in them, you have to know that they are on your side. To trust God you have to know He is on your side.

God is on your side – He is not angry with you. In the Old Testament we often see Him as a God of anger, but in the New Testament we see Him as a God of love. Yet the Bible tells us God is always slow to anger and abounding in love and that He never changes. God dealt with sin once and for all through the Cross, as Jesus took all the punishment for it, and God poured out all His anger against sin onto Him. His anger has been satisfied and He is not pouring anger out on us anymore, either as individuals or nations.

For God didn't appoint us to wrath, but to the obtaining of salvation through our Lord Jesus Christ.
(1 Thessalonians 5:9)

Jesus became sin for us and God poured out all His anger against sin on Him. And not just for those who would believe, but for everybody.

And he is the atoning sacrifice for our sins, and not for ours only, but also for the whole world. (1 John 2:2)

Our sins have been punished through Jesus and are now forgiven and God no longer remembers them. This was prophesied in the Old Testament –

"... for I will forgive their iniquity, and I will remember their sin no more." (Jeremiah 31:34b)

When we go to God and say, "Oh God, I've done it again," He answers, "What do you mean – again?" God is not holding anything against us. Justice has been done. Our sins have been punished, but it is not us that suffers the punishment – it was Jesus 2000 years ago.

God did not change His mind about sin at the Cross. He still hates sin, but now the need for us to be punished and suffer His anger has been satisfied by the Cross.

Much more then, being now justified by his blood, we will be saved from God's wrath through him. (Romans 5:9)

The Cross was enough: there is nothing we can do to add to it. It is all about what Jesus did, not what we do – how we measure up or how we perform. It is all about love and grace.

There is therefore now no condemnation to those who are in Christ Jesus. (Romans 8:1a)

But there is just one sin which Jesus said was not covered by the Cross and which cannot be forgiven – we call it the unforgiveable sin. This is a conscious, utter and permanent rejection of Jesus and His sacrifice and of His Holy Spirit. It is not a passing thought, a period of doubt or confusion or even a drifting away from God. It involves actively rejecting who Jesus is and what He has done, and knowingly reviling the Holy Spirit. The person who has committed it has –

... trodden underfoot the Son of God, and has counted the

blood of the covenant with which he was sanctified an unholy thing, and has insulted the Spirit of grace. (Hebrews 10:29b)

If someone is worried in case they have committed the unforgiveable sin, they have not done so. The person who has done so will have no remorse or concern about it at all. Someone who is willing for you to minister to them, by definition has not committed that sin, and you can tell them with complete confidence that all their sins are forgiven and God is not angry with them.

God is on your side – He wants you to be well. Many times when someone wants you to pray with them, it is about sickness. To have confidence to minister healing, you must understand what God's attitude towards sickness and healing is. Otherwise you have no place to start.

Do not decide what you think about healing by what you see or how you feel or the experience of others. Believe what God says. This is why I can write this, even though I still have some M.E. symptoms. I am not basing my teaching on how I feel or what my experience is or what the medical profession have told me, but on the truth of the Word of God. If you base what you believe about healing on what God says and refuse to be swayed by what you can see or how you feel, your belief in healing will grow and you will be much more likely to find it and will be more able to minister it effectively to others.

God wants us well physically, emotionally and mentally. He does not want us to suffer any kind of sickness or disability. On the contrary, He wants us free to live fruitful, abundant lives and to be able to serve Him effectively, unhampered by illness. Jesus defeated Satan and all his works including sickness and disability on the Cross – He carried all our illness so that we should not have to carry it ourselves, in just the same way as He carried our sins. Jesus –

> ... healed all who were sick; ¹⁷that it might be fulfilled which was spoken through Isaiah the prophet, saying, "He took our infirmities, and bore our diseases." (Matthew 8:16b-17)

In the Lord's Prayer, Jesus said to pray that God's will be done on earth as it is in heaven. We know that there is no sickness in heaven, so it cannot be His will that there be sickness on earth or Jesus would never have included this in His prayer. If someone is arguing with you about whether God sends sickness or not, this alone has to convince them, if they are willing to admit it.

We are not called to suffer in sickness for God. Jesus does tell us to take up our Cross. However, this does not apply to ill health, but to living daily in the truth that our old selves have been crucified with Christ.

> Those who belong to Christ have crucified the flesh with its passions and lusts. (Galatians 5:24)

It also applies to the willingness to suffer for the sake of the Gospel.

> ... all who desire to live godly in Christ Jesus will suffer persecution. (2 Timothy 3:12)

It is Satan who does not want people to be well. He wants them limited in what they can do and focused on themselves. He will use sickness to try and undermine a person's faith. When someone is healed, Satan will sometimes deceive the person into thinking they are still ill by imitating the symptoms of the sickness.

Ill health can be a direct attack from Satan or the result of living in a fallen world, picking up viruses and germs. It can be a failure to look after ourselves. It can be the result of sin, either personal or generational. It can be inherited. But ultimately all causes go back to Satan. And because Satan has been defeated on the Cross, we have the authority through Jesus over all sickness.

God can, however, work for our good during illness, but this does not mean God makes us sick or wants us sick. His ordained method of working in us is through His Word and His Holy Spirit and other loving Christians.

When you minister to someone who is ill, you can do so in complete confidence that the sickness or condition is not sent from God and that His will is that they be well and fully functioning. Do not be swayed by what you see or feel or by the experiences of other people with a similar sickness or condition. Be assured by the truth of God's Word and refuse to be moved from it in your thinking. You will then be able to help the person to grasp the truth too. I go into healing in more detail in chapter two.

God is on your side – He wants you to live a long life. When God created Adam and Eve, He intended that they should live forever. But once they had sinned, He brought in death so they would not have to live forever in a messed up world. Death was not a punishment, but an act of love. God then gradually reduced people's life span.

Various factors influence how long people may be expected to live –where they live and their personal situation. And individual people can also influence their life span by how they live. But God wants everyone to live a long and satisfied life. He says to the person who loves and follows Him –

"I will satisfy him with long life." (Psalm 91:16a)

But not everybody or even every Christian dies in God's time. It is not God who kills a baby or cuts a young person's life short in some tragic way. He does not send cancer to strike someone down. God's desire is that everyone dies simply because they are satisfied at the end of a long life. This means dying in old age peacefully, not in pain or suffering.

It is Satan who wants people to die early. The sooner he can end their life, the more chance there is of their dying unsaved. And he wants Christians to die early to limit the work they can do for God on earth. So when someone dies before their time, it is not God, but Satan who has killed them. Of course, for the Christian, his victory over the person is only momentary as they go straight to Jesus. However, the grief and pain of the person's loved ones remains and is Satan's handiwork, not God's.

"For I know the thoughts that I think towards you," says the LORD, "thoughts of peace, and not of evil, to give you hope and a future." (Jeremiah 29:11)

When you minister to someone who has been told they are going to die, you can do so in the complete confidence that God wants them to live a full span.

If God is for us, who can be against us? (Romans 8:31b)

If the Lord God Almighty is on your side, how can anyone or anything successfully come against you? It only can, if you let it. When things are difficult, determine to remember that God is on your side and that you are safe in that knowledge and belief.

God is always faithful to Himself and to His Word. We can totally rely on His promises. When you minister to someone, always expect God to touch the person and for the encounter to be positive. He is faithful and His desire for that person to be well and whole and free is greater than yours and even theirs.

Expect the healing, deliverance, freedom and restoration won on the Cross for them, to become reality in their body and life. Be confident in God's love for them and all He has done for them and wants to do for them.

You have just read some wonderful truths of who God is and what He is like. Having read them you can choose to dismiss them; you can choose to think how wonderful they are but doubt them; you can choose to believe they are true for everyone else but not necessarily for you (a common lie of Satan); or you can choose to believe God's truths and start to base your thinking, your words and your actions on them.

God is not going to make you believe – He has given you free will. But He is drawing you with His love. If you have had doubts about God and what He is really like, give in today and allow Him to draw you into His love, knowing He is on your side.

Read these verses out loud and allow God to speak to you. Let the truth of His Word settle in your heart and mind where it can work in you for your good, and build you up in your confidence in Him.

"I have loved you with an everlasting love. Therefore I have drawn you with loving kindness." (Jeremiah 31:3)

God so loved the world, that he gave his one and only Son, that whoever believes in him should not perish, but have eternal life. (John 3:16)

God commends his own love towards us, in that while we were yet sinners, Christ died for us. (Romans 5:8)

"For I know the thoughts that I think towards you," says the LORD, "thoughts of peace, and not of evil, to give you hope and a future."(Jeremiah 29:11)

God was in Christ reconciling the world to himself, not reckoning to them their trespasses. (2 Corinthians 5:19)

See how great a love the Father has given to us, that we should be called children of God! (1 John 3:1a)

God's love has been poured into our hearts through the Holy Spirit who was given to us. (Romans 5:5b)

If God is for us, who can be against us? (Romans 8:31a)
The LORD is on my side. I will not be afraid. (Psalm 118:6a)

The Lord is faithful, who will establish you and guard you from the evil one. (2 Thessalonians 3:3)

He will cover you with his feathers. Under his wings you will take refuge. His faithfulness is your shield and rampart. (Psalm 91:4)

The LORD is my light and my salvation. Whom shall I fear? The LORD is the strength of my life. Of whom shall I be afraid? [2] When evildoers came at me to eat up my flesh, even my adversaries and my foes, they stumbled and fell. [3] Though an army should encamp against me, my heart shall not fear. Though war should rise against me, even then I will be confident. (Psalm 27:1-3)

"Behold, I am with you always, even to the end of the age." (Matthew 28:20b)

For I am persuaded that neither death, nor life, nor angels, nor principalities, nor things present, nor things to come, nor powers, [39] nor height, nor depth, nor any other created thing will be able to separate (me) us from God's love which is in Christ Jesus our Lord. (Romans 8:38-39)

Chapter 2

Confidence in Jesus

In the last chapter, we said that in order to have confidence in someone, we have to know what they are like and how they think, act and react. We saw that we can have complete confidence in God and in His love for us – He loves us totally and unconditionally and He is on our side.

Now we are going to look at Jesus. The Bible tells us very clearly that He is not only God's Son, but God Himself. Jesus said –

"I and the Father are one." (John 10:30)

And He only did what He saw God doing. He said –

"... the Son can do nothing of himself, but what he sees the Father doing. For whatever things he does, these the Son also does likewise." (John 5:19)

This means that everything we learnt about God in the last chapter applies to Jesus too. Jesus was God on earth – God's love in action. The basis of all ministry is the fact that as Jesus died, He won the victory over Satan and all his schemes. Ministry is all about Jesus and what He won for us on the Cross.

Because Jesus was willing to give up everything for us, we can trust Him completely. He went through unimaginable pain and suffering – physical, mental, emotional and spiritual for us. It was all motivated by love. We can have complete confidence in Him because He demonstrated total, unconditional, sacrificial love for us – for each one of us personally, including you, and at immeasurable cost to Himself.

Greater love has no one than this, that someone lay down his life for his friends. (John 15:13)

The Cross stands at the centre of all history and it changed everything. It was the place where Jesus defeated Satan along with his works of sin, sickness, poverty and death.

To this end the Son of God was revealed: that he might destroy the works of the devil. (1 John 3:8b)

On the Cross, Jesus took the punishment we deserve so that we might come into an everlasting love relationship with God as our Father – forgiven, free, healed, made whole, blessed, lacking nothing and filled with His Holy Spirit. It is through the Cross that we can be assured of eternal life as we receive Jesus as our Lord and Saviour. It is only then that we become God's child.

Someone may ask you how they can become a Christian or ask you to help them accept Jesus.

... if you will confess with your mouth that Jesus is Lord, and believe in your heart that God raised him from the dead, you will be saved. [10]For with the heart, one believes resulting in righteousness; and with the mouth confession is made resulting in salvation. (Romans 10:9-10)

It is good if the person you are leading to Christ can form their own prayer, but if not, ask them to repeat what you say a sentence at a time. Make sure they know that salvation does not come as the result of saying certain words, but as the result of a sincere heart accepting Jesus in faith. You can use the simple approach of Sorry, Thank You and Please as in the prayer below. Before you start, explain what it means and why it is important.

"I am **sorry**, Lord God, for all the things I have done and said which are wrong, for all the things I should have done and didn't do, and for all my wrong thoughts and attitudes. **Thank You** Jesus, that you suffered all the punishment for all my sins. Thank You that I am forgiven because of Your sacrifice. Thank You that You rose from the dead and are alive for evermore. **Please** come and live in me, Jesus. I accept You as my Lord and Saviour."

When the person has sincerely prayed, assure them that they are forgiven and are now born again regardless of how they feel – what matters is their sincerity. Also assure them that the Holy Spirit now lives in them; they are a new creation in their spirit; and God is faithful – He will always be with them, He has promised to never leave them.

If you realise that you have never been born-again, or you are not sure, do not let this opportunity pass. Accept Jesus as your Lord and Saviour for yourself. If you have done that with a sincere and open heart before God, you are now born-again and can minister to others in the full confidence that you are God's child with His Holy Spirit living in you.

Jesus defeated all sin, sickness and poverty on the Cross. It was dealt with once and for all, and because of this, all the blessings of God, including forgiveness and healing are available to us. They already have our names on them. The job is done. It is not about what we do anymore; it is about what Jesus did. Our healing and the solution to all our problems already exist in the spiritual realm. As we minister, we are calling them into the physical realm so bodies, hearts and minds can be healed and difficulties overcome.

When we minister to people, we are not asking God to do what He has already done. For example, if we are ministering to someone who is full of guilt, we do not ask God to forgive them, but we thank Him for the forgiveness Jesus won for them on the Cross and we help the person to repent and receive their forgiveness. If we are ministering healing, we do not ask God to heal the person, but thank Him for the healing He has already won for them on the Cross and command it to manifest in the person's body.

As born-again Christians, the Holy Spirit lives in us with His full nature of love, joy, peace, patience, kindness, goodness, faith, gentleness, and self-control. The Holy Spirit has not left part of Himself outside – He is in us in His fullness. The fruit do not have to grow and develop as is often taught. They are mature, but we have to learn to allow them to flow and direct and influence us. So, for example, if we are ministering peace to a Christian, we do not ask God to give the person peace, but thank Him that they already have His peace and ask Him to help them to release it.

Ministry is far more about standing in what God has already done, than asking Him to do it.

_____

Jesus won our forgiveness on the Cross. Many people struggle with guilt and it can impact on every part of their lives. Jesus took all our sin, all our guilt and all our shame on Himself and He did it 'once for all'.

> ... *he did this once for all, when he offered up himself.* (Hebrews 7:27b)

He did it for all people – everyone who has ever lived, is living, and ever will live. He did it for all time – it stands in history at a specific time and will never need to be repeated. And He did it for all sins – past, present and future. If Jesus had only won forgiveness for past sins, He would have to go back to the Cross each time someone sinned and repented.

Every sin is forgiven, even those committed by non-Christians. When Jesus died, God knew every sin every individual person would ever commit, and every single one was forgiven through the punishment Jesus suffered. But we have to believe in what Jesus did for us, and receive the forgiveness He has won for us, for it to operate in our lives.

When you do something wrong and go to God feeling wretched, it does not surprise Him – He already knew all about that particular sin when Jesus died on the Cross and He punished it and forgave it then. Nothing surprises Him. He does not want you feeling guilty and ashamed – it is Satan that wants you to feel like that, because then you are less able to live life to the full and you become less effective in the work God has called you to do. Jesus said –

> *"The thief only comes to steal, kill, and destroy. I came that they may have life, and may have it abundantly."* (John 10:10)

However, sin does matter. It gives Satan an inroad into our lives to mess us up. And when we sin we hurt ourselves and often other people. But none of us is perfect, so what do you need to do when you sin? You do not have to ask God to forgive you – just confess (agree with Him that what you have done is wrong), repent (turn away from it), and receive your forgiveness.

Receiving the forgiveness does not mean it only becomes real at that moment. It was real two thousand years ago. But it can now work in you positively, as opposed to the sin working in you negatively.

If we confess our sins, he is faithful and righteous to forgive us the sins, and to cleanse us from all unrighteousness. (1 John 1:9)

God has to stay true to what happened on the Cross.

Of course, we all do, say and think things which are wrong without even realising, so there will always be sins which we do not repent of. But they do not cause us to lose our salvation or lessen God's love for us. Be assured that all your sins are forgiven. This is so important to grasp for your own growth, and also so you can minister this to others.

Jesus also won our prosperity. Today there are lots of people who are struggling materially for one reason or another. They may have lost their job, they may be in debt, there may have been a relationship breakdown, they may be facing big bills or struggling to support their family.

In *Deuteronomy 28* there is a list of blessings for those people who kept the law which God gave through Moses, and a list of curses for those who did not. Poverty in lots of forms is listed under the curses. It is not listed under the blessings at all; in fact abundance in all things is listed under the blessings. When Jesus died He took on Himself the whole curse of the law, including poverty, so that we could be free from it.

Christ redeemed us from the curse of the law, having become a curse for us. (Galatians 3:13a)

God won true prosperity for us through Jesus.

For you know the grace of our Lord Jesus Christ, that, though he was rich, yet for your sakes he became poor, that you through his poverty might become rich.
(2 Corinthians 8:9)

It is often said that this verse refers to spiritual riches only. God certainly wants us to be rich in spiritual things, however, if you look at the context of this verse, it is set in the middle of two whole chapters about money and giving.

The financial prosperity God has won for us is not about us having millions of pounds and extravagant lifestyles, a huge house and many expensive possessions. It is about us having enough to live comfortably and well without the fear and stress of financial problems, and also with enough over to be able to give generously into God's Kingdom, and help and bless others as Jesus tells us too. When you fully understand and believe in God's prosperity, you can confidently minister it to others.

And Jesus won our healing. Perhaps the most common reason people need ministry is sickness. Through Jesus' suffering and death, sickness was defeated and we are healed. The job is done in the spiritual realm. In the following verse, the tense of the verb is past –

You were healed by his wounds. (1 Peter 2:24b)

In the last chapter we saw how God wants us healed and we see this in action in Jesus. Jesus spent a lot of time on earth healing people and never inflicted sickness on anyone. On the contrary, He healed every single person who asked Him and was willing to receive. Often He healed every disease and every sick person in huge crowds. He was not making individual judgements about whether healing was appropriate, or the person deserved it. And He was doing only what He saw His Father doing. Jesus said –

"Most certainly, I tell you, the Son can do nothing of himself, but what he sees the Father doing. For whatever things he does, these the Son also does like wise."
(John 5:19)

People often want a let-out clause to explain why they are not healed which puts the responsibility on God. Arguments can be put in compelling spiritual ways. There are various wrong 'explanations' which are often given when someone is not healed. You will probably have heard some of them – you may have believed some of them, you may have said some of them yourself. This is not to condemn you or make you feel you have let people down. It is to help you see the truth so you can be confident in it from here on in.

You have to test everything against what the Bible says. And with healing, your focus must be on the New Testament or passages in the Old Testament which prophesy about Jesus, as it was on the Cross that the victory over sickness was won. Here are some wrong teachings about sickness –

'God's teaching you something through it.' Of course God wants to teach you, but the Bible tells us that His ordained way of teaching is through His Word, the Holy Spirit and other loving Christians.

'God uses sickness to make you a better person.' God wants you to grow as a Christian, but He never sends or prolongs sickness to do this. He can work in you in the middle of sickness, but He doesn't send it.

'God uses sickness to discipline you.' Sickness is listed in the curses of the law in *Deuteronomy 28* and God did punish people with sickness in the days of the law before Jesus, but He no longer does so, as we are forgiven and Jesus has set us free from the curse of the law.

'God heals in special times and moments,' and 'Healing is all in God's timing.' Jesus was always willing to heal – God's perfect timing for healing is always 'now'.

There are of course real reasons why healing may not come. Here are some of them –

Wrong teaching – some churches, books and ministries are teaching wrong ideas about healing, such as those listed above. They base their teaching on the evidence they can see in front of their eyes or on a Bible verse taken out of context or on Old Testament theology instead of on the truth of Jesus.

Satan – he does not want us to be well, but he can only mess us up as much as we will allow him to. We can resist him and all his lies in the name of Jesus.

Atmosphere – there is a huge atmosphere of unbelief in the western world. People generally will not even consider miracles and even many Christians doubt that they will actually happen. Atmosphere is significant and can stop healing. When a blind man from Bethsaida came to Jesus for healing, Jesus took him out of the village because it was a place of great unbelief and He wanted him away from that atmosphere. And then, having healed him, Jesus told him not to tell anyone back in Bethsaida about it. He knew they would be sceptical and could undermine the man's faith.

Lack of faith – a major reason is lack of faith for healing in either the sick person or those praying for them or both. *Mark 6:1-6* tells us that even Jesus could not heal many people in His home town of Nazareth, and He gave the reason for this as the people's unbelief. Many healings are not seen today because of the lack of faith for healing in an individual, a church, a place or even a country.

Method – the way Christians approach healing can be misguided. The Bible says to command healing in Jesus' name, yet many Christians pray to God, asking Him to heal them. Do not talk to God about the sickness, talk to the sickness about God.

Sometimes lack of healing cannot be explained, but that does not make the Bible wrong, it just means we do not fully understand. There are reasons why everyone is not healed instantly or why it never happens, but it is never God's fault. If someone asked for healing, Jesus healed them.

The churches and ministries where healing is seen regularly today are not the ones which teach that God may deny or delay healing, but those that teach that healing is always God's will and is already won through the Cross, and expect it to happen, or at least to start, now.

Never take what someone else says or writes about healing as true, whoever they are, unless you know it is backed up in the New Testament. If you believe wrong teachings, you are allowing in unbelief. You are then much less likely to see healing either in yourself or in those you minister to.

Choose to believe what Jesus taught and demonstrated about sickness and healing, not what experience or feelings may indicate. The truth of God's Word can bring all the healing and deliverance that you and anyone you minister to need.

But it is only as you believe it, that its truth will be confirmed to you. You can then have complete confidence in Jesus and all He has won for you on the Cross. And you can confidently share it with those you minister to.

JESUS' HEALING MINISTRY – THE PERFECT MODEL

If we have confidence in Jesus and all He has won for us and the people we minister to, then it follows that we should have confidence in the way He went about His healing ministry.

It is good to look at how Jesus healed people, so we can base our healing model on Him and not on our own or other people's ideas. Here are some aspects of the way He ministered. He never forced healing on anyone. He healed every single person who asked Him. He never turned anyone away. He never judged the person to see if they deserved to be healed. He never asked God if He wanted that person healed. He never told them the time was not right. He never said that God wanted to teach them something and when they had learnt it they would be healed. He never said sickness was a punishment – He did say it can sometimes come as a consequence of sin, but that is because sin gives Satan the opportunity to mess our lives up, not because God is punishing us.

Sometimes Jesus initiated ministry by approaching the person Himself. If you are filled with compassion for someone who is suffering, be aware that it might be God prompting you to minister to them if they are willing. On other occasions the person or people who needed healing approached Jesus and asked Him to heal them or someone else who was with them, and He responded to them.

Jesus was moved to heal and deliver by compassion. The Bible tells us so often that He saw someone's plight and had compassion on them. Sometimes it says that as He looked out over huge crowds, He had compassion on everyone and healed them all. Jesus had such a desire to see people set free and restored. But it was not sympathy. Sympathy is different from compassion. It can work against healing. Saying things such as "poor you" and "it is such a shame" leave people where they are and actually confirms them in their situation. Jesus saw the need and grieved that the person was in such a state and then did something about it. He brought them out of it into healing and freedom. That is compassion. We need to make sure, when we respond to what someone tells us, that we show love and compassion, rather than sympathy.

As Jesus ministered, He visualised the person who was sick as healed. The occasion this is made clear is when Jesus raised Jairus's daughter from the dead. He told the people who were mourning that she was not dead, but asleep. This was not yet physically true, but Jesus saw her with the eyes of faith and visualised her alive.

Jesus often commanded someone who was physically disabled in some way, to do something that was medically impossible. For example, He said to a man with a withered hand –

"Stretch out your hand." He stretched it out; and it was restored whole, just like the other. (Matthew 12:13b)

It was as the person responded in faith and obeyed the command that the healing came.

The Bible tells us Jesus often laid hands on people as He healed them. And He said of those who would be His followers, and that includes us –

"... they will lay hands on the sick, and they will recover." (Mark 16:18b)

Almost every time Jesus ministered healing it came instantly or as soon as the person obeyed Him in something He told them to do. But once the healing was not instant. After Jesus had laid hands on the blind man from Bethsaida, He asked him if he could now see. The man replied that he could see partly. So Jesus ministered again. Take heart that even Jesus had to minister twice on this occasion. It is good to ask someone if anything has happened after you have ministered to them. If not, do it again, just like Jesus did. We know that God always wants complete healing instantly, but faith plays a huge part and many healings take place gradually following ministry. Always encourage the person to expect healing and to stand firm in the truth that it is already won.

Jesus quite often gave advice to the person about whether to tell others about their healing or not. More often than not, He told the person not to say anything. Jesus was protecting them from coming up against unbelief which could undermine their faith. But once, Jesus did instruct someone to tell others what had happened. After he had delivered the Gadarene man of demons He told him to go home and tell his friends what had happened. Jesus must have known that they were open to believe what he said. When the man told them they marvelled. We need to discern when we minister healing to someone whether it would be wise or not for them to talk about it to others. If necessary, explain to them why it could be a problem, and suggest that they only share their healing with people who they know have faith for healing, at least for a while.

Healing at a distance was not Jesus' normal practice. There is no record of Him ever commanding long distance healing for someone when He was by Himself or just with His disciples, yet this is something that happens a lot in church circles. There are just three instances in the Bible where Jesus did heal someone who was not actually with Him.

Firstly, a nobleman came to Jesus and begged Him to go to his house to heal his dying son. Jesus spoke to him about faith and the man begged Him again. The way He did this must have shown Jesus that the man had faith, and He said to him –

"Go your way. Your son lives." The man believed the word that Jesus spoke to him, and he went his way.
(John 4:50b)

The father went home believing what Jesus had said and when he got there he found his son miraculously healed.

On the second occasion, a Roman centurion came to Jesus to ask Him to heal His servant. He did not ask Him to go to his house but said he believed Jesus could heal at a distance.

When Jesus heard it, he marvelled, and said to those who followed, "Most certainly I tell you, I haven't found so great a faith, not even in Israel." (Matthew 8:10)

He then said to the centurion –

"Go your way. Let it be done for you as you have believed." His servant was healed in that hour.
(Matthew 8:13)

The third time it was a Canaanite woman who came to Jesus and asked Him to deliver her daughter of severe demonization. After speaking with her, Jesus said –

"Woman, great is your faith! Be it done to you even as you desire." And her daughter was healed from that hour.
(Matthew 15:28b)

We can find three common denominators in these cases which can help us be confident about when it is appropriate to command long distance healing.

First, Jesus did not initiate any of these healings. In the three recorded cases all the healings resulted from someone approaching Jesus and asking Him to heal someone else in their household.

Secondly, in each case the person who approached Jesus was someone closely connected to the ill or demonized person, and they made direct contact with Jesus. The representative was not just someone who knew the sick person or had heard of them – it was someone who was part of their household, in these cases either a parent or a master.

Thirdly, Jesus made it crystal clear in every case that the faith of the person's representative brought about the healing. Faith is essential as we have already seen. This means that you cannot just command healing for people at random. There has to be a faith input from the person who is sick or from their close representative.

When we hear of a person who is suffering, we can pray that God will send someone to them to tell them about the victory Jesus has won for them over sickness. And we can pray that the sick person may come to understand God's truth that their healing is already won, and believe it and receive it in Jesus's name.

If someone comes to you and asks you to pray for healing for someone else, which is a very common occurrence, think – does the situation fit into the way Jesus did long distance healing? If so, then command the healing. If not, explain to the person about Jesus' victory over sickness. Pray with them that the sick person may be open to hear of what Jesus has done for them, so they are open to ministry themselves.

So many times Christians pray for healing for someone who is absent and then feel dispirited when nothing changes. Be discerning. When you follow Jesus' model, you can do so with complete confidence.

———————

Jesus trained His disciples as they watched Him heal and deliver people. He talked to them about it and answered their questions. And when they were ready, He sent them out in twos to do the same.

He did not give them instructions to make contact with Him before they healed someone to make sure it was appropriate. He did not tell them to pray to God about it. He did not tell them to get prayer back-up. He simply said –

"Heal the sick, cleanse the lepers, and cast out demons. Freely you received, so freely give." (Matthew 10:8)

He told them to just get on and do it, and that is what we as His disciples today need to do. Do not be tempted to wrap ministry up in religious talk or surround it with spiritual sounding qualifications.

Unlike the people the disciples healed before the crucifixion, the person you are ministering to has already had their sickness healed spiritually. God has done it. You are just commanding what has already been done to manifest in their body.

Jesus said to His disciples –

"For most certainly I tell you, whoever may tell this

mountain, 'Be taken up and cast into the sea,' and doesn't doubt in his heart, but believes that what he says is happening; he shall have whatever he says."
(Mark 11:23)

When you or someone who you are ministering to is facing a problem in life, the problem is the mountain. Jesus says to speak to the mountain and tell it to go. He does not say pray to God and ask Him to take it away. He refers to speaking directly three times in this verse. He really wanted His disciples to understand this and we need to understand it too. Do not talk to God about the problem, talk to the problem about God and what Jesus has done in winning the victory over it.

THE JESUS MODEL OF 3 PARTS

Jesus did not take much time at all when He healed and delivered people. He was very direct and to the point. But it is helpful to see the way He healed as having three separate parts. This will give you confidence as you follow Jesus' model, by giving you a framework in which to minister healing.

In part 1 Jesus connected with the person and established their faith. He established a relationship between the person and Himself. Sometimes He would ask a relevant question about the person or their problem. Sometimes He moved the person to another place or took control over who was present, in order to establish the right setting for faith for healing. Jesus often encouraged the person to have faith and believe. By the end of part 1, He had the information He needed and the person was in a place, both spiritually and physically, where they were able to receive.

In part 2 Jesus ministered to the person and as He did so, He no longer saw the person as sick, disabled or bound. He visualised the person as they would be – healed, free and whole. He allowed the Holy Spirit to work through Him as He commanded healing and deliverance. Sometimes He gave a specific command for the person to do something and it was as they obeyed, that they were healed.

In part 3 Jesus encouraged the person and gave any necessary advice. He often encouraged them by telling them that their faith had healed them. Sometimes He gave some practical advice to help them go forward. Often He gave them advice about whether to talk about their healing to others or not.

We are going to look at the example of Jairus' daughter being raised from the dead to help you see Jesus' 3 part model in action. Jairus had approached Jesus and asked Him to go to his house to heal his daughter.

In part 1 Jesus says He will go with Jairus, but as they are on the way, a report comes telling Jairus that his daughter has now died. Jesus reassures him and encourages him not to be afraid, but to have faith. He goes with Jairus to his house and chooses which disciples He will take in with Him along with Jairus and his wife. He finds that the room where the girl is lying is full of people wailing with grief. Jesus does not see the girl as dead, but as asleep – He is seeing in faith what will be true. When He tells this to the mourners, they ridicule Him and He turns them all out to get rid of a negative atmosphere of unbelief.

In part 2 Jesus ministered simply and directly to the girl, commanding her to rise up. She came back to life and sat up straightaway.

In part 3 Jesus gave advice about building up the girl's strength. He also told Jairus and his wife not to tell anyone what had happened. When Jesus had arrived at the house, He had found a palpable amount of unbelief and He did not want the girl or her parents' faith in Him and what He had done to be undermined.

I encourage you to put Jesus' example of healing ministry above any other that you have heard, read about or previously used. I am not saying they are all wrong – many of them will be fine. And God always honours the name of Jesus and responds to faith. But why follow a different pattern when we have the perfect model in Jesus.

Remember that Jesus' ministry was always short and to the point. We often feel that we need to make ministry a long session – it can feel more spiritual. Sometimes it is helpful, especially in emotional healing, but it is not Jesus' usual model. Use the following guidelines to help you to heal the Jesus way.

In part 1, connect with the person and establish their faith. Ask them what their name is if you do not know it, and tell them yours. Ask what they would like ministry for, if you do not already know. If you feel you need to understand more about the person's situation, ask straightforward questions. Tell the person that God loves them and wants them well. Tell them that Jesus has already won their healing for them on the Cross. Encourage them to have faith for healing.

In part 2, minister to the person. Lay hands on them – if possible lay hands on the affected part. Visualise the person as healed. Command healing in the name of Jesus. Address the problem by name and simply command it to go. Speak with authority. Use whichever of these examples best fits the situation – command anything that has invaded their body, such as cancer or a virus to leave and die; if part of the body is malfunctioning, command it to function perfectly; if the person has an injured or diseased or weak limb, command them to stretch it out; if the person has mobility problems command them to stand and walk; Ask the person if they are aware of anything happening. If something has happened, but the full healing has not come, command healing again and ask the question again.

In part 3, encourage the person and give any necessary advice. If healing has come, tell the person their faith has made them well and give God the glory. If the healing is only partial or not apparent or it is impossible to tell, assure them that God loves them, that He is on their side, and that their healing is already won. Encourage them to have faith that things will start to change and healing will fully manifest. If you feel there is some Godly advice that is needed, then give it.

You were healed by his wounds. (1 Peter 2:24)

You can have complete confidence in Jesus and all He won on the Cross and in the way He ministered to people. You can therefore have confidence that, as you minister the way He did, things will happen.

Chapter 3

Confidence in the Power

We have looked at how we can be confident in God and in Jesus. But for miracles to take place there has to be power. We need to understand the power God gives us, believe in it, and be confident in it and use it. We are going to look at three sources of Godly power – the Holy Spirit, the Word of God and the name of Jesus. And then we will look at faith which is the key that activates the power. Of course, we can only have God's power within us if we are born-again.

THE POWER OF THE HOLY SPIRIT

The Holy Spirit is God – He is the third part of the trinity. Jesus ministered in the power of the Holy Spirit, not in the fact that He was God.

> God anointed him with the Holy Spirit and with power, who went about doing good and healing all who were oppressed by the devil, for God was with him.
> (Acts 10:38b)

If Jesus ministered in the power of being God, we would not be able to do the same, but He said –

> "Most certainly I tell you, he who believes in me, the works that I do, he will do also; and he will do greater works than these, because I am going to my Father."
> (John 14:12)

It is because Jesus ministered in the power of the Holy Spirit that it is possible for us to do what He did. He descended on Jesus at His baptism and was the power Jesus used for all His miracles. He now lives in all God's people, teaching, directing, guiding, counselling, comforting, helping and empowering us. All true believers in Jesus have the Holy Spirit living in them. He is God's gift to them.

> *... do not you know that your body is a temple of the Holy Spirit who is in you, whom you have from God?*
> *(1 Corinthians 6:19a)*

The Holy Spirit is the Spirit of Truth. Jesus said –

> *"... when he, the Spirit of truth, has come, he will guide you into all truth." (John 16:13a)*

The Holy Spirit inspired the Bible, moving its writers to record faithfully all that He directed them to – this is why we can trust God's Word as absolute truth. He makes the Bible come alive as we read it, helping us to understand it on a spiritual level. He guides us into all we need to know in regard to spiritual matters.

He will also guide us as we minister, so we are able to minister effectively.

He is our Teacher and he reminds us of all we have read and heard of God and of Jesus.

> *"But the Counsellor, the Holy Spirit, whom the Father will send in my name, he will teach you all things, and will remind you of all that I said to you." (John 14:26)*

He is working in us to change us to make us more like Jesus.

But we all, with unveiled face seeing the glory of the Lord as in a mirror, are transformed into the same image from glory to glory, even as from the Lord, the Spirit.
(2 Corinthians 3:18)

When we do not know what or how to pray in a particular situation, the Spirit will intercede when we ask Him, and pray in our place. As we pray in tongues, it is Him praying through us exactly what He knows is needed.

... the Spirit also helps our weaknesses, for we do not know how to pray as we ought. But the Spirit himself makes intercession for us with groanings which cannot be uttered. (Romans 8:26)

The Holy Spirit will help you in all these ways as you minister if you allow Him to. He will show you the truth about the situation you are ministering into and what the person needs and how to proceed. He will remind you of things God has said in His Word so you can speak them out in the ministry situation. He can inspire you as you minister and help you to visualise the person set free from whatever their problem is.

The Holy Spirit will always work in you and through you if you are open to Him, but He will not force His way in. He may give you a word or phrase or a picture. He may give you a Bible verse. He will put a way to proceed in your mind. He may give you guidance to give to the person which is going to help them walk forward in faith.

If you do not know what to do when you are ministering,

silently ask the Holy Spirit to guide and help you – He will. Or you can openly invite the Holy Spirit to come into the person's situation at that moment in time. If you are not sure if the person would understand this, ask them if they are comfortable for you to invite the Holy Spirit. Explain that you will then both be quiet for a few moments. They will not then be worried, wondering what is going on, and will be able to focus on God. You do not need to beg the Holy Spirit – simply invite Him by saying, "Come Holy Spirit." He will come. If a way to minister settles in your mind, trust that it is His direction.

But to have the power of the Holy Spirit operating in and through you, you need to be baptised in the Holy Spirit. Jesus said –

> "But you will receive power when the Holy Spirit has come upon you." (Acts 1:8a)

The Holy Spirit comes to live in a person when they accept Jesus as their Lord and Saviour. However, Jesus talked to His disciples about a further experience than being born-again – one of empowering through baptism in the Holy Spirit.

It is the difference between having the pilot light on in a central heating boiler, and the whole boiler igniting as the valves open up so it is full of fire and is able to do its job of heating the house and the water. When you are born-again, the pilot light is lit – you have the Holy Spirit living inside you. But when you are baptised in Him, the valves open and the pilot light is able to light all the burners. You are then full of the fire and power of the Holy Spirit which you can use to bring about changes for the better in the people and situations around you. For some, this baptism occurs at the same time as they are born-again, but for many, it is a separate experience. And following this baptism, we need to ask and allow God to keep filling us with His Holy Spirit, so we can continually overflow to bless others.

Christians who have not been baptised in the Holy Spirit tend to struggle in their Christian walk and witness because they are largely doing it in their own strength. If you want to minister to others, it is essential that you are baptised in the Holy Spirit. You will have little power or gifting if you are not. You will struggle in your own strength and not achieve much.

Below are guidelines which will lead you into baptism of the Holy Spirit. You can also use them to lead others. They are based on three words beginning with A – Acknowledge, Ask and Accept. But remember, as with all Christian things, it is not about going through a form of words, but about being sincerely open to God and receiving with faith.

Acknowledge that you have no power of yourself and you need God's power to be able to serve Him, and that God has the power to give you through His Holy Spirit and wants to give it to you. **Ask** God for the fullness of the baptism of the Holy Spirit. **Accept** and receive the baptism in faith.

When you minister this to someone else, help them to understand the importance of living by faith, not feelings. Tell them not to rely on their feelings – being baptised in the Holy Spirit may be a wonderful emotional experience or they may feel nothing at first. But God is faithful and if they have sincerely opened themselves up to the Holy Spirit, the proof of something life-changing having taken place will show as time goes by.

Explain to them about the gifts of the Holy Spirit (see below) and that it is now possible for them to operate in them.

The Holy Spirit is God's gift to those who are born-again, and when you are baptised in the Holy Spirit, the power of the Holy Spirit can flow out of you in many different ways. The Bible calls these ways the gifts of the Spirit. It is possible for you to operate in all the gifts if you will step out in them. But God gives a specific gift or gifts to someone when He wants them to make that gift their main focus in serving Him. Someone who repeatedly operates in a particular area with ease and success has that particular gift from the Holy Spirit.

The Holy Spirit distributes these gifts as He determines, but the Bible tells us to desire the gifts, which implies that we can have some bearing on the gift or gifts He gives us. If you want to minister to others, desire the gifts which will help you to do so. You can find the main list in *1 Corinthians 12:7-11*. Some are of particular relevance to ministering – wisdom, knowledge, faith, gifts of healing, miraculous powers, distinguishing between spirits, prophecy and workers of miracles.

> *... if the Spirit of him who raised up Jesus from the dead dwells in you, he who raised up Christ Jesus from the dead will also give life to your mortal bodies through his Spirit who dwells in you. (Romans 8:11)*

What an amazing truth – think about it – the power that brought Jesus back to life lives in you through the Holy Spirit! Decide to believe it and allow it to bring healing to you and to the people you minister to.

THE POWER OF GOD'S WORD

God's Word is absolute truth. Because of this, we have to give it priority over our own experience, the experiences of others and the way the world looks at things. In every situation where we are looking for the truth, we have to go to the Bible. If we minister to people and they are not healed, our experience can tell us that God does not want them to be healed, or at least, not yet. But the Bible tells us differently. Which are we going to believe? We have to decide.

You will never find peace in making your experience the decider of truth. It will just lead to all sorts of doubt and confusion and can also lead to fruitless discussions and disagreements with other people. But when you make the Bible the decider of truth you have something of real worth to pass on to people and you can go forward and minister in confidence. You have to get this decided in your own life in order to be able to minister with success. It is not always easy, but the more you discipline your thinking to make the Bible the source of your truth, the easier it gets. When we understand and believe the truth of God's Word and live it out in our thoughts and in our actions and reactions, it will set us free. Jesus said –

"You will know the truth, and the truth will make you free." (John 8:32)

Because God's Word is absolute truth, it is also absolute power – it always was and always will be. God will always be faithful to what He has said and nothing can stand against it. His established principle of power in His Word is still at work today. It is therefore powerful to use verses and phrases from the Bible as you minister.

Every Scripture is God-breathed and profitable for teaching, for reproof, for correction, and for instruction in righteousness, [17]that each person who belongs to God may be complete, thoroughly equipped for every good work. (2 Timothy 3:16-17)

The Bible tells us that God's Word is itself health to our bodies.

My son, attend to my words. Turn your ear to my sayings. Let them not depart from your eyes. Keep them in the centre of your heart. For they are life to those who find them, and health to their whole body. (Proverbs 4:20-22)

Speaking God's Word over our bodies or someone else's is amazingly powerful. It is possible for a person to receive the help they need, including healing, simply by hearing the Word and allowing its truth to reach into their innermost beings.

He sends his word, and heals them, and delivers them from their graves. (Psalm 107:20)

And the Word of God is our weapon. It is –

… the sword of the Spirit, which is the word of God. (Ephesians 6:17b)

We need to follow Jesus' example. When Satan was tempting Him, He used Scripture to defeat him. Scripture is truth and Satan hates to hear truth.

It is always good to give people you minister to a verse, no matter what the ministry has been about. They then have a powerful weapon to use and a wonderful truth to stand on. Do not hesitate to share a verse from the Bible with someone you are ministering to because you think they already know it. It is always good for us to be reminded of all God has done, and the Holy Spirit can bring it alive in a fresh way and use it to bring healing, freedom and restoration.

Discern if the person you are ministering to is in a spiritual place where the Word can bear fruit. If they do not understand it, they cannot relate it to themselves; or if they do not believe it, it cannot help them; or if they do not determine to stand on it when temptation or trouble comes, it will not be of value to them.

> *… the word they heard didn't profit them, because it wasn't mixed with faith by those who heard.*
> *(Hebrews 4:2b)*

If necessary, help the person to understand what the verse means and how it relates personally to them, so they can feed on it and be nourished by it and allow its power to work in them.

> *"… so is my word that goes out of my mouth: it will not return to me void, but it will accomplish that which I please, and it will prosper in the thing I sent it to do."*
> *(Isaiah 55:11)*

Encourage the person to take hold of the verse, learn it, believe it, and base their thinking on it and determine to stand on its truth – it is the only way its power can work in their lives. Explain the importance of speaking God's Word out loud, especially when suffering or doubting or when under attack – it will confirm the truth to their heart as they hear it spoken out, and the devil also hears and trembles. It can help for the person to write the Bible verse out and put it up where they will keep seeing it. I stand in front of the mirror and declare the Word of God that I need to hear to myself.

If you do not know the exact wording of a verse or where it is in the Bible, use a concordance or digital search function to find it. Be honest and say that you are not sure where it is. Do not sell the person short because you feel embarrassed about not knowing the verse accurately. And write the reference down for the person to take away.

But be careful – the Cross changed everything and the victory over Satan was only won as Jesus died. Many prayers of the Old Testament are no longer relevant for us to pray today, living on this side of the Cross. Below are four of many examples. Explore others for yourself.

The Old Testament prayer in *Psalm 57:1a* said, *"Be merciful to me, God, be merciful to me."* But the New Testament truth in *1 Peter 2:10b* says, *God's people, who had not obtained mercy, but now have obtained mercy.*

The Old Testament prayer in *Psalm 38:21* said, *"Do not forsake me, LORD. My God, do not be far from me."* But the New Testament truth in *Matthew 28:20b* says, *"Behold, I am with you always, even to the end of the age."*

The Old Testament prayer in *Psalm 6:2b* said, *"LORD, heal me."* But the New Testament truth in *1 Peter 2:24b* says, *You were healed by his wounds.*

The Old Testament prayer in *Psalm 6:1* said, *"LORD, do not rebuke me in Your anger."* But the New Testament truth in *Romans 8:1* says, *There is therefore now no condemnation to those who are in Christ Jesus.*

For the many things God has won for us through Jesus, our prayer should no longer be "Please," but "Thank You." For instance, our prayer today is not "Please be with me," but "Thank You that You are always with me." Do not ask God to do things He's already done, but thank Him for what He's done and help the people you minister to, to believe and receive what Jesus has won for them.

At the end of this book you will find Bible verses which you can use in ministry, arranged under subject headings.

THE POWER OF THE NAME OF JESUS

God has given us all authority to heal and command demons to go in the name of Jesus. There is infinite power in His name. God has exalted it to the very highest place. It is of supreme importance and value and everything ultimately has to bow to it, including sickness and demons.

Therefore God also highly exalted him, and gave to him the name which is above every name, [10]that at the name of Jesus every knee should bow, of those in heaven, those on earth, and those under the earth. (Philippians 2:9-10)

Whatever you or someone you are ministering to is facing has a name. Cancer, M.E., fear, depression, arthritis, poverty and everything else has to bow at the name of Jesus. When Jesus sent His followers out to heal and deliver people, they were thrilled with the power of His name –

The seventy returned with joy, saying, "Lord, even the demons are subject to us in your name!" (Luke 10:17)

We need to be bold as we minister to people in Jesus' name, trusting and expecting that as we step out in faith, using the power we have been given, miracles will happen. Jesus has already defeated sickness on the Cross and it cannot stand against His name, but it is faith in His name which will make the healing manifest physically. After Peter had healed a lame man and everyone was amazed to see the man leaping and praising God, he explained to them –

"By faith in his name, his name has made this man strong, whom you see and know." (Acts 3:16a)

When we minister, we are not trying to defeat the sickness or any other problem – that has already been done. We are commanding what already belongs to the person to manifest in their body in the name of Jesus, and encouraging them to receive it by faith. Jesus said –

"These signs will accompany those who believe: in my name they will cast out demons; they will speak with new languages; [18]they will take up serpents; and if they drink any deadly thing, it will in no way hurt them; they will lay hands on the sick, and they will recover." (Mark 16:17-18)

FAITH

God won everything for us through grace. We could never deserve or earn what He has done for us. Jesus went to the Cross because of God's unconditional love for us. He gave up everything so we could have it all. That is grace. But the blessings only become ours as we receive them in faith.

Even our faith is a gift from God, but, it is up to us to take hold of it and use it.

> ... by grace you have been saved through faith, and that not of yourselves; it is the gift of God, [9]not of works, that no one would boast. (Ephesians 2:8-9)

Faith is essential for the power the Holy Spirit, God's Word and the name of Jesus to operate. Jesus taught that we need to have faith to see results. It is the key that activates the power. Read this verse again –

> "By faith in his name, his name has made this man strong, whom you see and know." (Acts 3:16a)

The power came through the name of Jesus, but the healing came through the man's faith in Jesus' name. The name of Jesus has the power, but it has to be believed in.

Jesus says it is faith which is spoken, not just thought, that will move the mountain.

> "Most certainly I tell you, whoever may tell this mountain, 'Be taken up and cast into the sea,' and doesn't doubt in his heart, but believes that what he says is happening; he shall have whatever he says." (Mark 11:23)

As you minister, speak directly to the problem in the name of Jesus and have faith that it will move. Remember, do not speak to God about the problem, speak to the problem about God and what Jesus has done in winning the victory over it.

Imagine a thermometer with faith at the top and unbelief at the bottom – that's what most Christians think they have with their reading fluctuating between the two. But it is not the case – we have two thermometers. One is called faith and one is called unbelief and they operate individually. So it is possible for our faith reading to be high and our unbelief reading to be high too. We all know that we believe, and yet we also know it is possible to have some doubting thoughts alongside. The father of a boy with an evil spirit recognised this and said to Jesus –

"I believe. Help my unbelief!" (Mark 9:24b)

Build your faith up by reading God's Word and focusing on His love and all you have because of Jesus, and knock your unbelief on the head by refusing to entertain doubting thoughts and refusing to see things the way the world does. Determine to find your truth in God's Word and feed on it, whatever is going on around you that seems to be saying the opposite. The more you do it, the easier it becomes. Renew your mind so your faith increases and your doubt and unbelief decreases.

Do not be conformed to this world, but be transformed by the renewing of your mind. (Romans 12:2a)

———————

You do not need to ask God for power – if you are born-again and baptised in the Holy Spirit, He has already given it to you – you have already got it. You have the Holy Spirit within you, you have the Word of God, you have the Name of Jesus, you have faith as a gift from God. You do not have to ask for the power or wait for the power. You do not have to wait for God to 'show up'. Jesus said just get on with it –

> *"Heal the sick, cleanse the lepers, and cast out demons. Freely you received, so freely give." (Matthew 10:8)*

It is as we obey this that miracles happen. And miracles lead to revival. If we simply get on with what God has told us to do and heal people and raise the dead, we will not have to think about revival – it will come. Be confident in the power you have, and release it and step out in it.

The power that we have from God does not just work by itself, we have to use it. The Bible tells us that God is able –

> *... to do exceedingly abundantly above all that we ask or think, according to the power that works in us.*
> *(Ephesians 3:20)*

God can work through us according to how much we use the power He has put within us.

For the power of the Holy Spirit to work in ministry, you have to believe in it and trust it and allow it to flow out of you to the other person.

For God's Word to work in power you have to believe it and speak it out. It cannot work in the other person's life if they do not hear it.

You have to use the name of Jesus spoken out loud, for its power to work.

For your faith to bring about healing and deliverance and freedom, you have to renew your mind so you can get rid of unbelief, and speak your faith out and put it into action. And you have to encourage the person you are ministering to to have faith too. Then God's power will work.

Have confidence that you have all the power you need to minister to others, because God has given it to you. You do not have to earn it, you do not have to ask for it – you just have to believe in it and use it in faith. Be bold and step out in it and see people healed, set free and made whole.

Chapter 4

Confidence in Yourself

To minister effectively you have to have confidence in yourself. If you have no confidence, you are going to be focused on yourself – you are going to be anxious about what you say and do. You are going to doubt that God will work through you.

So how can we have confidence in ourselves and yet remain humble before God? The answer is, we do not have confidence in our own abilities – we have confidence in Jesus in us and through us.

The only reason you can have true confidence in yourself is because of who you are in Jesus and because of what God has done for you through Jesus. You might feel you are not clever enough or wise enough to minister to others, but God is! And He wants to work through you as you minister.

If you feel confident because you are good at taking control, are articulate, assess situations quickly and clearly etc. it will help you go through the motions of ministry, but it will be of no help in seeing people healed, delivered and made whole. But you can have complete confidence in yourself because of Jesus. He said –

"These signs will accompany those who believe: in my name they will cast out demons; they will speak with new languages; [18]they will take up serpents; and if they drink

any deadly thing, it will in no way hurt them; they will lay hands on the sick, and they will recover." (Mark 16:17-18)

The Bible tells us that, as born-again believers, we are new creations.

Therefore if anyone is in Christ, he is a new creation. The old things have passed away. Behold, all things have become new. (2 Corinthians 5:17)

This used to really puzzle me – I knew it was true because it said so in the Bible, but I also knew that I was far from perfect. To understand it, we have to know that we are made up of three distinct parts – spirit, soul and body *(1 Thessalonians 5:23b)*. We know that our bodies did not become new creations when we were born-again. And although God's light shone into our minds and started to change us, we know that our souls (our minds, wills and emotions) are not completely new creations either.

But when we were born-again, our old spirit was crucified with Christ and God gave us a brand new perfect spirit – this is the very essence of who we are and it is where we are a new creation. Our new spirit is with us for eternity. It is inappropriate for a born-again Christian living today after Jesus' death and resurrection, to ask God to give them a new spirit – He's already done it. When I understood this, so many things fell into place and I could sing 'I am a new creation' with confidence and joy.

Do not ask God to give a new spirit to a born-again believer you are ministering to – He's already done it. Instead explain to them what God has done, thank Him for it and help them to believe it and stand on it.

Look at this amazing verse –

> ... *he who is joined to the Lord is one spirit.*
> *(1 Corinthians 6:17)*

Because your spirit is perfect, it is joined with the Holy Spirit as one spirit within you. God has done it. And then look at this verse –

> ... *as he* (Jesus) *is, even so we are in this world.*
> *(1 John 4:17b)*

We are like Jesus right now here on earth! We know we are not yet like Jesus in our thoughts and our emotions – it is our spirits which are like Him. These two verses are truly amazing. Take some time to dwell on them and let their truth settle into your heart and mind never to be dislodged.

In our spirit we are made perfect – a new creation which can never be spoilt. In our spirit we have perfect faith, knowledge, power and victory; our spirit always believes and is always rejoicing. You can have complete confidence that in your spirit you are a new creation.

As we minister, we do so in partnership with God. We are doing His work, not our own. We minister in the name of Jesus and in the power of the Holy Spirit and the Word of God, not in our own wisdom and strength. It is obviously wrong to say ministry is all about us and nothing about God, but it is also wrong to say it is all about God and nothing about us. Jesus told His followers to go out and heal people. He told them to just do it and by implication, if they did not do it, the people would not be healed. But we can only do it in the power of God. He wants to work through us.

Of ourselves we can do nothing, but we are not empty vessels or channels for God to work through as is often said. We are full – we are filled with the Holy Spirit and the power of God – that is why God can use us. It is important to get the balance. It is us doing God's work.

For we are God's fellow workers. (1 Corinthians 3:9a)

God wants us to partner with Him in bringing healing, deliverance and blessing to others – it is such a privilege! Have confidence in yourself as a fellow worker with God.

It is amazing to think that we are in a better position to heal and deliver today than the disciples were before Jesus died, because Satan and sickness had not been defeated then and the power of the Holy Spirit had not been given. But today, we have the knowledge that Satan and sickness are defeated and healing is already won in the spiritual realm and we have the power of the Holy Spirit within us. I believe this is why Jesus promised us –

"Most certainly I tell you, he who believes in me, the works that I do, he will do also; and he will do greater works than these, because I am going to my Father."
(John 14:12)

Have confidence that you can do what Jesus did and even more, because Satan is defeated and you have the Holy Spirit within you.

God has given us power. I talked about this in detail in chapter 3, but just to remind you – if you want to minister to people it is vital that you are baptised in the Holy Spirit. (See pages 46-48)

Now to him who is able to do exceedingly abundantly above all that we ask or think, according to the power that works in us. (Ephesians 3:20)

God's promise that He can do more than we can even imagine is 'according to the power that works in us'. It is not God working independently of us, but it is Him working through us as we step out in faith using the power He has given us. Remember, you do not have to ask God for power – you have the Holy Spirit, you have God's Word, you have the name of Jesus. Instead, ask Him to help you understand it, release it and use it.

We have been given authority. In the beginning God had authority over everything. But after He had created human beings, He gave them authority over the earth.

The heavens are the heavens of the LORD; but the earth has he given to the children of men. (Psalm 115:16)

God did not give any right or power to Satan to rule over the earth – He gave it to man. But when Adam and Eve succumbed to Satan's schemes and sinned, they yielded their God-given authority over to him. God had given authority to physical human beings, and to be true to His own Word, He could not just take it back to Himself. It was not because He did not have the ability to do so, but because of His integrity.

God wanted to restore authority to people. He did this by coming to the earth Himself as a physical man. By defeating Satan and all his schemes on the Cross, He restored dominion over the earth to the man Jesus. This is why it was essential that Jesus was a man and why He referred to

Himself as 'the Son of Man'. Jesus won back the authority God had given mankind and which man had handed over to Satan. Now, as the man God, Jesus had all authority in heaven and in earth. After His resurrection He said –

"All authority has been given to me in heaven and on earth." (Matthew 28:18)

In the following verse He then said to His disciples –

"Go, and make disciples of all nations, baptising them in the name of the Father and of the Son and of the Holy Spirit, teaching them to observe all things that I commanded you." (Matthew 28:19)

Jesus was sharing the authority he had won back from Satan with His followers and that includes us. However, it is no longer given to us solely as it was to Adam and Eve – it is shared with Jesus.

Satan is coming against us with lies and deception, but we are able to take these thoughts captive and resist him. We need to recognize that we are the ones who now have authority and power. The victory comes in knowing the truth of our authority from God, standing on it and speaking it out in Jesus' name. Because of Jesus, you can have complete confidence in your God-given authority as you minister.

UNDERSTANDING SATAN AND HIS METHODS

To be confident in ministering it is important to have some understanding of Satan and how he works. As we minister, we are engaging in a spiritual battle and Satan is the enemy.

The first rule of battle is said to be, 'know your enemy'. So what do we know about Satan?

> *"The devil ... was a murderer from the beginning, and doesn't stand in the truth, because there is no truth in him. When he speaks a lie, he speaks on his own; for he is a liar, and the father of lies." (John 8:44b)*

The only power Satan really has against us is lies and deception – this is always his starting point. He did not come against Adam and Eve with physical force – he did not come as an elephant and threaten to squash them or as a lion and threaten to tear them apart. He came as a snake, so he could use cunning. This is still the way he works today, lying to people so that when they become deceived, he is able to take some control and cause problems in their lives. The way we are told to stand against Satan is in our thinking.

> *For though we walk in the flesh, we do not wage war according to the flesh; ⁴for the weapons of our warfare are not of the flesh, but mighty before God to the throwing down of strongholds, ⁵throwing down imaginations and every high thing that is exalted against the knowledge of God and bringing every thought into captivity to the obedience of Christ. (2 Corinthians 10:3-5)*

It is only as we believe the lies Satan feeds us and succumb to his deception that he is able to move against us. The armour God gives us to protect ourselves is all designed to defeat deception. If we know the truth of God and the truth of the victory Jesus has won over Satan and his demons, we can stand on it and live it out. Resist Satan and he will have to flee.

Be subject therefore to God. Resist the devil, and he will flee from you. (James 4:7)

As born-again believers, we now have power and authority over Satan. We should not be afraid of Satan – Satan is afraid of us!

It is important to keep Satan in perspective. Many Christians today see Satan as having immense power, but the truth is, he is a defeated enemy with very limited power, far less than we have as children of God.

… greater is he who is in you than he who is in the world. (1 John 4:4b)

But it is important to acknowledge his existence and realise that he is at war with us. To live as though he is of no account, is as misguided as crediting him with more power than he has.

Be watchful. Your adversary, the devil, walks around like a roaring lion, seeking whom he may devour. (1 Peter 5:8)

Satan is not really a lion, but he pretends to be – he walks round like a lion. He pretends he is a physically powerful and violent animal in order to frighten people. And notice in this verse that Satan has to look for people he can attack or inhabit. He cannot 'devour' just anyone. Those who stand in the truth of Jesus and His victory and resist Satan are protected. His activities are not to be ignored, but to be dealt with in the name of Jesus, in the sure knowledge that he is an already defeated enemy. Jesus commanded his disciples to go and cast out demons.

*He called the twelve together, and gave them power and
authority over all demons. (Luke 9:1a)*

You may find in ministry that someone has a demon and
needs deliverance. It could be a Christian or a non-Christian.
You have the power of God to command demons to leave in
the name of Jesus. But deliverance can get a bit difficult
sometimes as Satan tries to resist. If you feel you do not
know how to proceed, simply bind the demon in Jesus'
name – command it to be quiet and not to hurt the person.
You do not need to shout, but you do need to use a voice of
authority. You can then explain to the person that, if they
are willing, you would like to ask someone else to minister
with you. Choose someone who you know has experience of
deliverance. That person will have no more power than you
have, but their experience will help them to understand
better what is going on and how to approach the ministry.

Do not look for demons in every ministry situation or
presume that a demon is the cause of every problem, but be
aware of the possibility. Remember, Satan is defeated and
the power in you is far greater than the power he has. You
have the power that raised Jesus from the dead living in
you! You can have confidence in yourself because Jesus is in
you and He has won the victory.

RIGHT THINKING

We all know that having or lacking confidence is all to do
with how we think. To have confidence in ourselves, we
have to get our thinking based on the truth of God's Word. I
keep saying this because it is so important.

Our spirit is new and perfect, but we know full well that our souls, where we think, feel and make decisions, are not. God calls us to transform ourselves through the renewing of our minds. Our aim should be to bring our mind into line with our perfect spirit.

People often think they have little or no control over what they think. But *Romans 12:2* shows us that it is possible to change how we think.

Do not be conformed to this world, but be transformed by the renewing of your mind. (Romans 12:2a)

Real transformation takes place as we renew our minds and start to think God's way, refusing to be swayed by the world's thinking or by what we see and feel. Remember we need to be –

... throwing down imaginations and every high thing that is exalted against the knowledge of God, and bringing every thought into captivity to the obedience of Christ. (2 Corinthians 10:5)

It is an on-going process and it will only be completed when we go to heaven, but it is our responsibility to start and continue the process here on earth.

Sometimes we do not know what to think about a situation – we only have to ask God, and He will give us His wisdom.

But if any of you lacks wisdom, let him ask of God, who gives to all liberally and without reproach; and it will be given to him. ⁶But let him ask in faith, without any doubting, for he who doubts is like a wave of the sea, driven by the wind and tossed. (James 1:5-6)

God promises to give wisdom to anyone who asks, but He says it is really important that we then trust Him to give it, and that we stop tossing the situation around in our mind and continue to fret about it. We need to learn to put this into practice – as with all Christian disciplines, the more we put it into practice, the easier it gets.

There are two decisions which are important to make when we ask God for His wisdom. We need to decide to believe that He will give it to us, and then we need to decide not to entertain any doubts about it. We cannot rely on our feelings, but if we have this truth firmly rooted in us, then it is there for us to stand on when we need it. We can then also pass it on in ministry. Often someone you are ministering to will need God's wisdom in their situation.

The more we bring our thinking into line with God's thinking, the more confident we can be. It is a discipline and takes effort. It is much easier to sit back and let your feelings control you, but there will be no peace that way. Determine to be transformed by the renewing of your mind, so you can walk further into the victory Jesus has won for you and be able to confidently lead others in it too.

Ministering to someone is not only about miracles – it is also about leading the person into the truth so they can renew their minds and stand on the truth and so find more and more victory in their life.

One of the most significant things we can do to renew our minds is to start to see ourselves the way God sees us – to know who we are in Jesus. God wants us to be sure of who we are as a result of all Jesus has done for us, and He wants us to receive that truth by faith.

Many Christians find this difficult and instead, they base their identity on who they think they are, or on who they think other people think they are. But it is only as we fully realise our identity is found in Jesus alone that we can have inner peace and true confidence.

It is easy to believe the lies Satan tries to feed us. He will use any means he can through our own thoughts, through others or through the media to knock us down. When you hear or read or see anything that makes you feel worthless or useless or ordinary, resist it. It is Satan's work. God wants to build you up, but He needs your co-operation to do so.

A true realisation of who you are in Jesus is a major key to being confident and effective when you minister. And if you are secure in who you are in Jesus, you can pass it on to others and help them to believe and receive it too.

Below are twenty Biblical statements which can build you up in faith in who you are in Jesus, if you choose to believe what they say. They do not describe what you are like, but who you actually are. Of course, for them to be true, you have to be born-again.

I have adapted each of them in two ways. Use the first adaptation of each one to declare the truth to someone you are ministering to, or use the second to declare it to yourself. Following them is an explanation.

Declare these statements out loud. As you speak your ears hear and the Word can enter your mind and heart, causing your faith and your confidence to grow.

Who you are in Jesus   and   **Who I am in Jesus**

1. You are a new creation. The old things have passed away. Behold, all things have become new.
1. I am a new creation. The old things have passed away. Behold, all things have become new.

When you were born-again, God gave you a brand new perfect spirit. It can never be corrupted or tarnished. The old has gone, the new has come. *(2 Corinthians 5:17)*

2. You are a temple of God, and God's Spirit lives in you.
2. I am a temple of God, and God's Spirit lives in me.

In the Old Testament, God lived in the tabernacle and then the temple in Jerusalem. But now you are His temple and He lives in you by His Spirit. *(1 Corinthians 3:16)*

3. You have been crucified with Christ, and it is no longer you that lives, but Christ lives in you.
3. I have been crucified with Christ, and it is no longer I that live, but Christ lives in me.

Your old fallen spirit was crucified with Jesus and now you have a brand new spirit which is the real you, and Jesus Himself lives in you by His Holy Spirit. *(Galatians 2:20a)*

4. You are joined to the Lord and are one spirit with Him.
4. I am joined to the Lord and am one spirit with Him.

Your new spirit is one with the Lord – it can be united with Him because He has made it perfect. *(1 Corinthians 6:17)*

5. As Jesus is, even so you are in this world.
5. As Jesus is, even so I am in this world.

Your spirit is not in the process of changing or developing. It is perfect and in your spirit you are just like Jesus right now on earth. *(1 John 4:17b)*

6. Because you have received Jesus and believed in His name, God has given you the right to be God's child.
6. Because I have received Jesus and believed in His name, God has given me the right to be God's child.

As Christians we do not think about having rights the way the world does, but we have the most wonderful right of all – that of being God's child. *(John 1:12)*

7. You have received the Spirit of adoption, so you can call God, "Abba! Father!"
7. I have received the Spirit of adoption, so I can call God, "Abba! Father!"

In biblical times, only the wealthy formally adopted children because it was a costly process. And they only made the outlay for a child they really wanted. God paid everything so He could adopt you – that is how special you are, that is how much He loves you and wanted you to be part of His family. *(Romans 8:15b)*

8. You are a child of God, through faith in Christ Jesus.
8. I am a child of God, through faith in Christ Jesus.

God wanted you to be His child so much, that He gave you the gift of faith which you could use to believe in Jesus as your Lord and Saviour and so become His child. *(Galatians 3:26)*

9. Because you are a child, you are an heir: an heir of God and a joint heir with Christ.
9. Because I am a child, I am an heir: an heir of God and a joint heir with Christ.

Because you are a child of God, you are His heir. Everything He has is yours – all the blessings, all the victory, and eternal life with Him as a member of His family. *(Romans 8:17a)*

10. You are a child of light and a child of the day.
10. I am a child of light and a child of the day.
God is not ashamed of you – He wants you to live in His light for all the world to see. *(1 Thessalonians 5:5a)*

11. Jesus doesn't call you a servant, for a servant doesn't know what his lord does. But He has called you His friend, for everything that He heard from His Father, He has made known to you.
11. Jesus doesn't call me a servant, for a servant doesn't know what his lord does. But He has called me His friend, for everything that He heard from His Father, He has made known to me.
God has shared His all with you. He has opened your eyes to His mysteries because you are so special to Him. He has done it because you are not a servant, but a friend – the friend of Jesus Himself! *(John 15:15)*

12. You are an individual member in the body of Christ.
12. I am an individual member in the body of Christ.
You are part of Christ's body and you fit perfectly into the place God has created especially for you.
(1 Corinthians 12:27)

13. You are the salt of the earth.
13. I am the salt of the earth.
You are so significant as God's child that you have the capacity to effect the world – you can preserve the good, you can melt the hard heart, you can increase and improve the flavour of people and situations around you.
(Matthew 5:13a)

14. The LORD has made you the head, and not the tail.
14. The LORD has made me the head, and not the tail.

This was one of the blessings of keeping the Old Testament law and all God's blessings were fulfilled for you through Jesus. The tail has to follow where the head leads. You do not have to be dragged around by someone or something else wherever they want you to go. You are the head and in Jesus can set your own course. *(Deuteronomy 28:13)*

15. You are the light of the world.
15. I am the light of the world.
Because Jesus shines in you, you light up the world and make it possible for people to see the truth and find their way to Jesus. *(Matthew 5:14a)*

16. You are God's workmanship.
16. I am God's workmanship.
You are the very handiwork of God, created by Him for His pleasure. God created the world and the plants and animals and birds and fish by the power of His Word. But He chose to create you from the earth, moulding you with His own hands to be loved by Him. *(Ephesians 2:10a)*

17. You are Christ's ambassador.
17. I am Christ's ambassador.
Ambassadors represent someone important. They do not hide away trying to melt into the background. They make sure that they do the work entrusted to them in a way which is faithful to the person they represent. You are an ambassador of Christ. Hold your head up as you live your life. God has chosen you to represent Him wherever you go. *(2 Corinthians 5:20a)*

18. You are God's fellow worker.
18. I am God's fellow worker.
God has chosen you to work with Him – what a privilege! He

wants you to share in what He does – that is how significant you are to Him. *(1 Corinthians 3:9a)*

19. You are a member of God's chosen people, a royal priesthood, a holy nation. You belong to God.
19. I am a member of God's chosen people, a royal priesthood, a holy nation. I belong to God.

God has chosen you to be set apart as His child – a member of His family with all the privileges that come with that including royalty and holiness. *(1 Peter 2:9)*

20. You are a citizen of heaven.
20. I am a citizen of heaven.

Jesus has prepared a place for you to live with Him forever and He has given you citizenship of heaven in advance – that is how sure He is of His love for you and His desire to have you with Him always. *(Philippians 3:20a)*

We have to take personal responsibility and choose to believe who we are in Jesus. It is the only way to real confidence in ourselves.

Be aware that some people you minister to will only be wanting an instant experience, without either the understanding or the determination to go forward and keep their faith alive and active on their own. Of course, we praise God for the wonderful times when we feel His touch directly, but it is important to understand that we and the people we minister to, need to base our Christian walk on the truth of God and what He has done through Jesus. We must learn how to sustain our experience of God in daily living – His presence is always with us. And understanding and believing who we are in Jesus is crucial in being able to do this.

But you, beloved, keep building up yourselves on your most holy faith, praying in the Holy Spirit. Keep yourselves in God's love. (Jude 1:20-21)

God is always wanting to shower you with His love, but if you sit back and just wait for the feelings, they may never come. If you live in the truth of the knowledge of God's love for you and who you are in Jesus, the feelings will follow along. Choose to humbly believe who God says you are. That is the way to peace and true confidence.

Satan does not want ministry to succeed. If he starts putting thoughts in your head as you are ministering like, 'Who do you think you are doing this?' or 'Nothing will happen,' refuse to listen. Thank God in your heart for who you are in Jesus and just get on with the work God has equipped you to do.

You will find that one or more of these 'I am' verses are often powerful in ministry. You could go through them with the person, or if you discern that one particularly relates to their situation, focus on that. Give them the relevant references and explain to them how powerful it is to speak God's Word aloud. Encourage them to speak these truths out over themselves and believe them and refuse to think negative thoughts about themselves anymore.

Knowing God's promises and believing them personally is also very significant in getting our thinking right.

For however many are the promises of God, in him is the "Yes." (2 Corinthians 1:20a)

God's Word has so many promises and they have all been fulfilled and made available through Jesus' death and resurrection to everyone who will believe them and receive them. Really believing these promises are true for you and basing your thought life on them will transform you from someone who is prone to fear, doubt and stress into someone who is strong and confident and at peace.

Read the following promises out loud and allow the truth of God's Word to minister to you in your thinking and in your heart. Let it build you up in confidence.

I have arranged the verses under ten subject headings. Every verse will build you up in Jesus, but if you struggle in a particular area, focus on the verses in that category regularly, and let them minister to you with God's truth and love. Again, I have adapted the verses so you can declare them either to someone else or to yourself.

God's Promises for You   and   **God's Promises for Me**

1. Fear

- For God didn't give you a spirit of fear, but of power, love, and self-control.
- For God didn't give me a spirit of fear, but of power, love, and self-control. *(2 Timothy 1:7)*

- The LORD is your light and your salvation. Whom shall you fear? The LORD is the strength of your life. Of whom shall you be afraid?
- The LORD is my light and my salvation. Whom shall I fear? The LORD is the strength of my life. Of whom shall I be afraid? *(Psalm 27:1)*

- No weapon that is formed against you will prevail; and you will condemn every tongue that rises against you in judgement.
- No weapon that is formed against me will prevail; and I will condemn every tongue that rises against me in judgement. *(Isaiah 54:17a)*

- Greater is he who is in you than he who is in the world.
- Greater is he who is in me than he who is in the world. *(1 John 4:4b)*

2. Loneliness or isolation

- God will in no way leave you, neither will He in any way forsake you.
- God will in no way leave me, neither will He in any way forsake me. *(Hebrews 13:5b)*

- Jesus is with you always, even to the end of the age.
- Jesus is with me always, even to the end of the age. *(Matthew 28:20b)*

3. Depression

- Jesus came that you may have life, and may have it abundantly.
- Jesus came that I may have life, and may have it abundantly. (John 10:10b)

- God alone is your rock and your salvation, your fortress. You will not be shaken.
- God alone is my rock and my salvation, my fortress. I will not be shaken. (Psalm 62:6)

- God raised you up with him, and made you to sit with him in the heavenly places in Christ Jesus.
- God raised me up with him, and made me to sit with him in the heavenly places in Christ Jesus. *(Ephesians 2:6)*

4. Doubt

- Jesus says to you, "Therefore I tell you, all things whatever you pray and ask for, believe that you have received them, and you shall have them."
- Jesus tells me that all things whatever I pray and ask for, if I believe that I have received them, I shall have them." *(Mark 11:24)*

- If you lack wisdom, ask of God, who gives to all liberally and without reproach, and it will be given to you.
- If I lack wisdom, I will ask of God, who gives to all liberally and without reproach, and it will be given to me. *(James 1:5)*

5. Anxiety

- Your God will supply every need of yours according to his riches in glory in Christ Jesus.
- My God will supply every need of mine according to his riches in glory in Christ Jesus. *(Philippians 4:19)*

- In Jesus you may have peace. In the world you have trouble; but cheer up! Jesus has overcome the world.
- In Jesus I may have peace. In the world I have trouble; but I chose to cheer up! Jesus has overcome the world. *(John 16:33)*

- He who didn't spare his own Son, but delivered him up for you, how would he not also with him, freely give you all things?
- He who didn't spare his own Son, but delivered him up for me, how would he not also with him, freely give me all things? *(Romans 8:32)*

6. Guilt

- Christ redeemed you from the curse of the law, having become a curse for you.
- Christ redeemed me from the curse of the law, having become a curse for me. *(Galatians 3:13a)*

- Being therefore justified by faith, you have peace with God through our Lord Jesus Christ.
- Being therefore justified by faith, I have peace with God through my Lord Jesus Christ. *(Romans 5:1)*

- In Jesus you have your redemption, the forgiveness of your sins.
- In Jesus I have my redemption, the forgiveness of my sins. *(Colossians 1:14)*

- Much more then, being now justified by his blood, you will be saved from God's wrath through him.
- Much more then, being now justified by his blood, I will be saved from God's wrath through him. *(Romans 5:9)*

- There is therefore now no condemnation to you who are in Christ Jesus.
- There is therefore now no condemnation to me who am in Christ Jesus. *(Romans 8:1a)*

7. Feelings of Inadequacy

- You are like a tree planted by the streams of water, that produces its fruit in its season, whose leaf also does not wither. Whatever you do shall prosper.
- I am like a tree planted by the streams of water, that produces its fruit in its season, whose leaf also does not wither. Whatever I do shall prosper. *(Psalm 1:3)*

- For him who knew no sin he made to be sin on your behalf; so that in him you might become the righteousness of God.
- For him who knew no sin he made to be sin on my behalf; so that in him I might become the righteousness of God. *(2 Corinthians 5:21)*

- In Jesus you are made full, who is the head of all principality and power.
- In Jesus I am made full, who is the head of all principality and power. *(Colossians 2:10)*

- Blessed be the God and Father of your Lord Jesus Christ, who has blessed you with every spiritual blessing in the heavenly places in Christ.
- Blessed be the God and Father of my Lord Jesus Christ, who has blessed me with every spiritual blessing in the heavenly places in Christ. *(Ephesians 1:3)*

- Be confident of this very thing, that he who began a good work in you will complete it until the day of Christ.
- I am confident of this very thing, that he who began a good work in me will complete it until the day of Jesus Christ. *(Philippians 1:6)*

8. Feeling Incapable

- God is able to do exceedingly abundantly above all that you ask or think, according to the power that works in you.
- God is able to do exceedingly abundantly above all that I ask or think, according to the power that works in me. *(Ephesians 3:20)*

- You can do all things through Christ, who strengthens you.
- I can do all things through Christ, who strengthens me. *(Philippians 4:13)*

9. Feeling Vulnerable

- God has established you in Christ and anointed you and also sealed you, and gave you the down payment of the Spirit in your heart.
- God has established me in Christ and anointed me and also sealed me, and gave me the down payment of the Spirit in my heart. *(2 Corinthians 1:21-22)*

- Be persuaded that neither death, nor life, nor angels, nor principalities, nor things present, nor things to come, nor powers, nor height, nor depth, nor any other created thing will be able to separate you from God's love which is in Christ Jesus your Lord.
- I am persuaded that neither death, nor life, nor angels, nor principalities, nor things present, nor things to come, nor powers, nor height, nor depth, nor any other created thing will be able to separate me from God's love which is in Christ Jesus my Lord. *(Romans 8:38-39)*

10. Lack of confidence

- Jesus says to you, "You didn't choose me, but I chose you and appointed you."
- I didn't choose Jesus, but He chose me and appointed me. *(John 15:16a)*

- If God is for you, who can be against you?
- If God is for me, who can be against me? *(Romans 8:31b)*

- You know that all things work together for good for you who love God, for you who are called according to his purpose.
- I know that all things work together for good for me who loves God, for me who am called according to his purpose. *(Romans 8:28)*

- In all things, you are more than a conqueror through him who loved you.
- In all things, I am more than a conqueror through him who loved me. *(Romans 8:37)*

- Now thanks be to God, who always leads you in triumph in Christ.
- Now thanks be to God, who always leads me in triumph in Christ. *(2 Corinthians 2:14a)*

If any of these verses have really spoken to you speak them to yourself through the days ahead. Write them out and prop them up where you can see them. Do what I do – look at yourself in the mirror and declare the truth of the verse to yourself. I tell myself the truth in the mirror and say, "Katherine, it is truth – believe it!"

When you are ministering, if you discern that someone's thinking is not Word-centred, talk to them about the truth of God's Word and how all His promises are fulfilled in Jesus. Explain that they need to base their thinking on God's truth, rather than on their own experience or the experience of others. If they are born-again, help them to see who they are in Jesus, and how God has made everything available for them to live in victory. Help them to make a decision to believe who God says they are, not who they or others think they are, and to receive all He has done for them, and trust Him for all He is doing and wants to do for them. This is a huge step forward in walking in victory.

All through this chapter I have encouraged you to see yourself the way God sees you and the way you are in Jesus. Decide to believe it and not to be swayed by anything that tries to say the opposite – your own negative thoughts, the words or actions of others, the way the media portrays people or the way the world thinks.

Being confident in who you are in Jesus will impact every area of your life, including when you are ministering to people. Choose to believe what God says – be confident and experience the truth setting you free, and through you, the people you minister to.

Chapter 5

Giving Confidence to the Other Person

So far we have found that we can have complete confidence in God, in Jesus and in His power, and we have seen how we can have confidence in ourselves in Jesus.

Now we are going to look at how we can give that same confidence to the people we minister to. We want to build them up in their understanding of, and faith in, God and what Jesus has won for them. And part of doing that is giving them confidence in us, so they will not be worried about us and are able to focus on God.

Being a Christian is not about just having head knowledge or following rules or going through rituals – it is not about going to church every Sunday; it is not about taking communion; it is not about spending time each day praying or reading the Bible. All these things are good and will help us grow and experience more of the love of God, but when we make them into rules that we must obey, we are putting ourselves back under the law. We are saying that what we do affects how God sees us, how much He loves us, whether He will answer our prayers or not.

Being a Christian is about being in a Father/child relationship with God. Many people believe in God – so does Satan. But allowing God into our hearts and serving Him out of love, rather than duty, is relationship and it is what God wants and what is God's best for us. When we know we are secure in our relationship with God, we will want to go to church, take communion, pray and read our Bible.

Do not presume that someone you are ministering to is born-again because of an intellectual belief or a good Christian habit such as going to church regularly. We need to help them to come into relationship with God, receiving Jesus at a real personal level. That is the best way to give them confidence.

LOVE

An essential part of stepping into the victory Jesus has won for us is believing in and experiencing the amazing love God has for us as individuals. We do not deserve it, we can do nothing to earn it – God loves us totally unconditionally and nothing can separate us from His love. Only when you know you are loved by God can you really love Him back and start to minister His love to others. We are set free from the law and now live under grace, but Jesus gave us a new commandment of love. He said –

"A new commandment I give to you, that you love one another. Just as I have loved you, you also love one another." (John 13:34)

This love commandment is not a restricting one, but a life-giving one which frees us and others as we live it out –

"If a man loves me, he will keep my word. My Father will love him, and we will come to him, and make our home with him." (John 14:23)

It does not mean we have to love others in order for God to love us. It means that if we have no desire to love others, it proves we are not truly born-again and Jesus does not live in us. Our actions prove our faith. And as we love others we are also loving God. Jesus said –

> *"Most certainly I tell you, because you did it to one of the least of these my brothers, you did it to me."*
> *(Matthew 25:40)*

Jesus perfectly demonstrated selfless love when He died on the Cross in our place. He also showed us the way of love and service during His earthly life. For example, when He washed the disciples' feet *(John 13:3-17)* He was willing to take the place of a servant in order to meet the needs of others.

Our first aim when we minister to someone should be to build them up in an understanding of, and faith in, God's love for them. Everything we do in ministry must be done in love. We are then revealing God's heart to the person. Love is full of compassion – it has a desire to see them set free from whatever holds them back. Love has to be central to ministry. If, after we have ministered to them, the person has a deeper understanding of God's love, we have helped them enormously and brought pleasure to the heart of our Father God.

Love is not weak and we must not use it as an excuse to avoid difficult issues with people. Love is bringing people out of sin, not ignoring it. The truth will set them free if they allow it to. Real love will want to lead them out of sin and into freedom and wholeness. If we compromise out of a concern for, or fear of, the person's reactions, we are selling them short before God. We need to be –

... speaking truth in love. (Ephesians 4:15a)

We must speak the truth, but we have to speak it in love, not condemnation.

When you really love someone, you do desire the best for them, and this is God's attitude towards us. He longs for us to know Him as our loving Father and live the life which He has planned for us – the best life to lead.

It is easy to want healing and restoration for someone you love, but sometimes you can come across a person who is hard to love. If someone like this asks you to minister to them, silently ask God to help you to see them as He sees them, and allow His love to flow through you.

The most important thing anyone can do in response to God's love is to accept Jesus as their Lord and Saviour. There is no relationship with God, no Christian life and no eternity with God without it.

If the person you are ministering to is not born-again, explain to them what Jesus did for them and see if they are willing to accept Him as their Lord and Saviour. This is loving them and is more important than any healing or resolution of their problems. Better a painful, difficult life on earth for a few decades and eternity in heaven in peace and joy, than a happy, pain free life on earth and eternal punishment.

Make sure the person has a sincere desire to be born-again from their heart, and that they understand what they are doing and its significance for their life. If they are willing, lead them to Jesus.

Bringing someone to salvation is the most wonderful thing we can do for them, but we cannot force or persuade them – God never does that.

"I have drawn you with loving kindness." (Jeremiah 31:3b)

We need to follow God's way and encourage the person in loving kindness.

If you will confess with your mouth that Jesus is Lord, and believe in your heart that God raised him from the dead, you will be saved. [10]For with the heart, one believes resulting in righteousness; and with the mouth confession is made resulting in salvation. (Romans 10:9-10)

Make sure the person believes sincerely in their heart and ask them to speak it out loud. If they are not sure how to do it, ask them to repeat a line at a time after you. You can use the model of 'Sorry', 'Thank You', 'Please'. The details are in chapter 2 on page 24. Encourage them that they are now a child of God and build them up in faith. Help them to decide not to base their understanding on their feelings, but on the truth of God. Being a child of God with a true understanding and experience of God's love for them through Jesus, will give them more confidence than anything else we can do.

FAITH

I have talked a lot about faith through this book and I am going to do so again. The Bible tells us –

… by grace you have been saved through faith, and that

not of yourselves; it is the gift of God. (Ephesians 2:8)

It is only through faith that we can respond to God's grace. Before we were born-again, God gave us the gift of faith when we were seeking Him, so we could believe in Him and receive our salvation. Now we are born-again, we still use our faith to receive from God all the blessings that He has for us. He has provided everything that we need, but it is through our response, our faith, that we receive it. Only when we believe it, can we receive it. And only when we receive it, can we pass it on to others.

Jesus said that faith is the only thing needed for healing. Many times He told someone that their faith had made them well. Faith has to be present for healing. When Paul saw a crippled man, he looked at him and –

… seeing that he had faith to be made whole, [10]said with a loud voice, "Stand upright on your feet!" He leaped up and walked. (Acts 14:9b-10)

Paul acted because he could see the man had faith for healing. Build up the person you are ministering to in their faith before you command healing. This may be a simple word to which they whole-heartedly respond, or it may involve a long discussion as the person seeks to understand and believe. Do not skip it – Jesus always encouraged people to believe as He ministered to them. As their faith rises, so their confidence will grow in things changing. If someone does not believe God wants them well and that Jesus has won their healing for them, do not command healing. Instead, explain to them the Bible truth that they are already healed in the spiritual realm and God wants them healed physically. Encourage them and build them up in this truth if they are willing. If they respond with faith, you can then command healing in Jesus' name.

Jesus said that we also need to have faith for the practical things in life, such as food and clothing. Material needs are a common reason for someone wanting ministry. Help the person to have faith in God's promise to provide all that they need. It is only when they believe that they can receive.

My God will supply every need of yours according to his riches in glory in Christ Jesus. (Philippians 4:19)

Laying hands on the person as we minister can stimulate faith and transmit power. Anointing the person with oil is also powerful – in the Bible it is a symbol of the Holy Spirit.

They cast out many demons, and anointed many with oil who were sick, and healed them. (Mark 6:13)

Always encourage faith by assuring the person of God's love and of the fact that He has the answer to any and every problem they may have. Jesus said –

"For most certainly I tell you, if you have faith as a grain of mustard seed, you will tell this mountain, 'Move from here to there,' and it will move; and nothing will be impossible for you." (Matthew 17:20b)

God put physical laws in place when He created the world, such as the laws of gravity and inertia and these laws are constant – they never change. In the same way He established the spiritual law of faith *(Romans 3:27)* which also will never change – it remains constant and can be depended on absolutely. Below are six principles of God's law of faith. By understanding these ourselves, we can stand on them as we minister and this will increase the faith of the person we are ministering to, and so build up their confidence in God.

So faith comes by hearing, and hearing by the word of God. (Romans 10:17)

Faith comes by hearing God's Word. If people do not know God's truth from His Word, they cannot have faith in it. As you minister to someone, equip them with Bible verses which will build up their faith and help them to stand on what He has done for them, is doing and wants to do. God's Word has the power to instil faith.

Jesus answered them, "Have faith in God. ^{23}For most certainly I tell you, whoever may tell this mountain, 'Be taken up and cast into the sea,' and doesn't doubt in his heart, but believes that what he says is happening; he shall have whatever he says." (Mark 11:22-23)

Faith has to be spoken out. Jesus taught that we have to speak our faith out to see it bring results. He says it is faith which is spoken, not just thought, that will move the mountain. As you minister, speak directly to the problem in the name of Jesus.

... faith, if it has no works, is dead in itself. (James 2:17)

Faith without works is dead. We can never earn God's love or our salvation by our works – by what we do. We have to receive it by grace through faith. But the natural outcome of faith is to seek to live to please God. If someone says they have faith, but live a selfish life, we are right to doubt their faith. It is not works that produce faith, but works prove our faith exists. Really understanding this can bring a real sense of relief to someone who is struggling, trying to earn God's love. Help them to walk into this truth and their confidence in being able to receive from God will grow.

"Therefore I tell you, all things whatever you pray and ask for, believe that you have received them, and you shall have them." (Mark 11:24)

Faith brings results. Jesus tells us to visualise what we have asked for as already ours. This is faith in action – believing for what we cannot see. The promises can then become reality. Help the person you are ministering to, to see themselves already healed and restored and their difficulties resolved.

Unforgiveness can short circuit faith. Forgiveness is central to the Christian life. Jesus taught his disciples about it on many occasions. He made it very clear that without receiving forgiveness from God there can be no relationship with Him. And when we have truly received our forgiveness, the result will be a desire to forgive others. Forgiving is not always easy, but it is possible. If it was not, Jesus would not have told us to do it. He then wants us to go further and choose not to think about the way people have hurt us anymore. It is for our benefit. This is what God does concerning our own sin. He had prophesied in the Old Testament that He would -

"... be merciful to their unrighteousness. I will remember their sins and lawless deeds no more." (Hebrews 8:12)

It helps to realise that when people hurt us, it is Satan working through them to try and beat us down. Jesus demonstrated this when Peter tried to turn Him away from the Cross. He turned to Peter but rebuked Satan, saying –

"Get behind me, Satan!" (Matthew 16:23a)

When we obey God and forgive others, He can heal the hurt and help us not to think about it. Forgiving someone who has hurt us opens the door to receiving our healing. The person may not be willing to be reconciled or they may have died, but the command is still for us to forgive them in our hearts before God. Forgiving does not automatically mean restoration of the relationship – we may need wisdom from God about whether to continue to be in contact with the person or not.

People who need ministry can often be struggling with receiving and/or giving forgiveness and they need to understand this teaching. If we fail to help them with this, we are limiting what God wants to do in their lives. Jesus said –

"Whenever you stand praying, forgive, if you have anything against anyone; so that your Father, who is in heaven, may also forgive you your transgressions."
(Mark 11:25)

He is not saying that we will lose our salvation if we do not forgive everyone everything. But if we are truly born-again and know we have received our own forgiveness from God, we will have a desire to forgive others even when it is difficult. If someone refuses to even consider forgiving, it probably means that they have not been born-again. It indicates a hard heart which cannot take hold of their own forgiveness which Jesus has won for them on the Cross.

Discern as you minister, if there is any significant area of unforgiveness in the person which could short-circuit and limit their faith in what God has done and wants to do for them. Talk to them about it and help them to understand more of how God loves them and has forgiven them. Build them up in their own forgiveness and encourage them to be willing to forgive others.

The sixth principle is – unbelief can cancel out faith. Someone may have faith for God to heal and resolve their problems, but if they also have unbelief, that can cancel out their faith and they will then struggle to see God at work in their lives. Jesus said we only need faith the size of a mustard seed. So, presuming the person does have some faith, the question is not so much, 'Do they have enough faith?' but rather, 'Is there any unbelief in them alongside their faith?' Faith is crucial, but unbelief is significant in a negative way.

Remember that we do not have one thermometer with faith at the top and unbelief at the bottom. We have two thermometers. One is called faith and one is called unbelief and they both operate at the same time. When unbelief exists alongside faith, it can cancel out the faith we have. Even Jesus could not heal many people in His home town of Nazareth because of their unbelief.

He could do no mighty work there, except that he laid his hands on a few sick people, and healed them. ⁶He marvelled because of their unbelief. (Mark 6:5-6a)

The disciples had a crisis of confidence when they were unable to drive a demon out of a boy.

Then the disciples came to Jesus privately, and said, "Why weren't we able to cast it out?" ²⁰He said to them, "Because of your unbelief. For most certainly I tell you, if you have faith as a grain of mustard seed, you will tell this mountain, 'Move from here to there,' and it will move; and nothing will be impossible for you. ²¹But this kind doesn't go out except by prayer and fasting."
(Matthew 17:19-21)

The last part of Jesus' reply has often been taken to mean that this particular kind of demon will only go out by prayer and fasting. But think about it – if the name of Jesus will not bring it out, then why should something that we do, be able to. It would make our prayer and fasting more powerful than the name of Jesus! Jesus gives the reason that the demon would not leave in *verse 20*. He said it was because of their unbelief. Something that the disciples could see happening before their eyes brought unbelief into their minds and their faith was not able to operate. And Jesus was saying that this kind of unbelief can only be extinguished by prayer and fasting.

We all have had doubts at some time. If we listen to doubts for long enough, they will set in as unbelief. We must recognise doubting thoughts as soon as they come into our mind. Satan wants to keep us doubting – resist Him with the Word of God and he will flee. It is essential that we believe in and trust God's Word, not our own understanding. Unbelief in us can limit what God wants to do through us.

Be aware that it is possible for someone to limit what God can do for them by believing negative words spoken to them by someone else. This can be especially powerful when the person speaking is someone with human authority. An example would be a doctor telling a patient that their condition is incurable. This will presumably be true from a scientific medical viewpoint, but we are inviting God into the person's situation and He has already healed them in the spiritual realm through the death and suffering of Jesus. So what the doctor says is not true in the spiritual realm and therefore does not have to be true in the physical. Make sure the person understands this and help them to get rid of their unbelief and have confidence in what Jesus has done.

Trust in the LORD with all your heart, and do not lean on your own understanding. (Proverbs 3:5)

As you minister, seek to discern if there is any unbelief in the person which can cancel out their faith. Listen as they speak – what is in their heart will show itself in what they say or how they say it. Unbelief can take away any confidence that they might have in God and in ministry.

Help them to knock their doubts on the head by focusing on God's love for them and all He has done for them through Jesus. Reaffirm them in the truth of God and His desire for them to be whole. Use Scripture to build them up in God's faithful promises and all He has won for them on the Cross and in who they are in Jesus. Explain to them about resisting Satan's lies with the Word of God. All this will build them up in confidence in God.

I have talked about love and about faith – they go hand in hand – they build each other up. In everything you do as you minister, do it in love. Love builds up faith as people respond to it, and as their faith rises, their love for God will too.

PRACTICAL WAYS TO GIVE CONFIDENCE

It is important to minister within a framework of good practice for the physical and emotional safety and protection of yourself and of the people you minister to. In doing so, you also protect the reputation of God's church. Love and respect for the person you are ministering to will dictate a lot of good practice, but it is good to think about some specific things. Below are ten points. They are all helpful in giving the person confidence in you, so they can then relax and focus on God and what He wants to do.

If you know in advance that you are going to be ministering to someone, make sure you have some tissues handy. It is not unusual in ministry for the person to start crying. It can be the Holy Spirit touching them in an emotional area which needs healing. It can just be the relief of handing their problem to God. But with tears goes a runny nose, and this is embarrassing. Quietly putt a tissue in their hand – it will solve the problem for them straightaway so they can refocus on God.

If you are ministering privately, it is good to do so with someone else. It protects you and gives you accountability. But do not make a rule out of this – ministry can often happen spontaneously, and ministry from one trusted individual can be very special and helpful. However, If you are by yourself, it is wise not to minister to someone of the opposite sex who is not a family member. If you know in advance that you are going to be doing some deliverance ministry, explain to the person that you would like to ask someone else along who you know has experience in that area.

Act naturally – do not do weird things. All the healing examples in the New Testament are of Christians speaking clearly and straightforwardly. If you do not know that the person knows about tongues, do not just start speaking in tongues yourself. If you feel God is directing you to do so, explain to the person what you would like to do and ask them if they are comfortable with it. Your aim is for the person to be focused on God and what He has for them, not losing confidence because of concerns about the way you are acting or speaking.

The Bible teaches us to lay hands on people as we minister to them. It does not say to hover hands over, but to lay hands on. So, as you do so, make contact, but never push the person. If they fall, it must be the Holy Spirit's doing, not yours. If the person feels in any way manipulated, you will lose any confidence that they had in you and therefore in the ministry. When ministering for physical healing, it is good to lay hands on the affected part if possible, as there is a build-up of faith as the part is touched. But we need to know the person is comfortable with this. If you are not sure, ask them.

People have very different attitudes towards physical contact and you need to be sensitive about it. One person may really respond to a big hug or a literal shoulder to cry on. Someone else may feel their space is being invaded, and if you try to hug them they will become self-protective and have negative thoughts about the ministry before you have even begun. If you do not know the person, err on the side of caution. Ask them if they are happy for you to put your hand on their arm, shoulder or head as you minister. This helps them to feel they are being respected and that they can trust you. If you know the person, it is much easier of course, but still be sensitive to the individual. Be especially careful if you are ministering to someone of the opposite sex.

Talk with the person during ministry. If you are not sure if they are used to being ministered to, explain what you are going to do and ask if they are happy about it. You do not want them worried about the fact that you have put your hand on their head, you want them to be looking to Jesus. Continue to explain what you are going to do throughout the ministry time, so they can have confidence in you and relax. Whatever the person's understanding of ministry may be, talk with them before and during ministry, as appropriate. You will need to explain God's truth about their situation to them and build them up in faith. Even if they already know it, tell them again. It will confirm what they know and encourage their faith and confidence in God.

Do not be afraid of moving between ministry and dialogue. If what is happening is real, there is no need to be concerned about breaking an atmosphere. If it is a man-made atmosphere it is achieving nothing anyway. If it is of God, it will not be affected by relevant conversation. As you talk, use everyday language. Try not to use Christian jargon unless you are certain the person understands it. Explain anything they do not understand. Always speak encouragingly and without manipulation, motivated by love.

When you are ministering, your focus must be on God and on the person you are ministering to, not on yourself. If the person tells you about something that you have also gone through in your own life, it is tempting to tell your own story. Even in ordinary conversation, it can be very frustrating when you are sharing something with someone and they take over and tell their story. Of course there is a place for you to say how God has helped you in a similar situation, but keep it as brief as possible. When you have done so, tell them that you have mentioned it to encourage them, and make sure the focus is straight back on them. This will give the person confidence that you are listening to them and not thinking about your own experience.

If someone falls in the spirit, catch them if possible. Let them down gently and make sure they are comfortable and feel safe. If they do not understand what is happening, tell them that this is a work of the Holy Spirit and encourage them to relax so they can continue to have confidence in the ministry and receive from God.

For people to have confidence in us as we minister, we need to match our talk generally with our ministering – both need to be faith-filled. What we say is very powerful in the impact it has on both ourselves and other people. The impact can be for good, but it can also be for harm, even though that is not our intention. Following ministry with negative talk, either immediately or at a later time, can cancel out its effectiveness and will not honour God or what He wants to do. It will also limit faith in the people who hear us. Do not get drawn into speaking about the person's issue at a human level after you have ministered to them. Keep redirecting them onto God and what He has done.

The last and one of the most significant areas in giving someone confidence is maintaining confidentiality. It is really important to keep everything that you hear in ministry confidential. If you start to tell other people about it, you are breaching the person's trust. If they hear you have talked about it to someone else, their confidence in you and in ministry will instantly be wiped out. I cannot emphasise this enough. Even if what you hear is common knowledge, do not initiate conversations about it yourself with anyone else. Child abuse or neglect has to be reported by law. If this is shared with you, gently explain to the person that you have to tell someone else. Talk to your church leadership to find out what you should do. Although it is important to include this information, I have never known it to arise personally.

———————

Whatever happens when you minister, build up the person's faith in what Jesus has done and encourage them to walk out in that faith. If you have commanded healing, encourage them to go forward knowing that it is already won in the spiritual realm and expecting it to manifest in their body, whatever the doctor or anyone else says. Give them Bible verses which they can stand on. Encourage them to keep their focus on Jesus and what He has done and on God's love, rather than on their own experience or the experiences of others.

If they have been able to have confidence in you, they will have been free to focus on God and this is what we want. We want the people we minister to, to have full confidence in God and in all that Jesus has won for them, and in who they are in Him.

Chapter 6

Confident to Minister

God is love. The Bible makes it clear that without love we are nothing and the one commandment Jesus gave us was to love. We know that love gives confidence and confidence increases love. When someone really loves us, it gives us confidence in them which frees us to love them back. This increases their confidence in us and their love for us grows. We then feel more confident in them and so it goes on – an ever upward spiral of love and confidence with Him.

God's love for us can never increase because it is already total and infinite, but as we receive His love, our confidence in Him grows and that helps us to love Him and receive more of His love, and so we progress in that upward spiral of love and confidence.

THE CIRCLE OF LOVE

God loved us from before creation. He always knew there was going to be a 'you' and the same is true for everyone. And it is because He loves us that we can love Him back. When we love Him and come into that wonderful love relationship with Him, we have a desire to share that love with others. As we minister to people and tell them the Good News, they can then respond to God and receive His love for themselves and start to love Him back in their own relationship with Him. It is a circle of love – God loves us, we pass His love onto others and they come to love Him.

When God created the world He did so by the power of His Word, but when He created man He formed him out of the dust of the earth with His own hands. He then formed woman out of one of Adam's ribs, again with His own hands. He did not want us to just come into existence, He wanted to mould and shape us Himself, pouring His love into us as He made us in His own image. We did not evolve – we are uniquely made, set apart from the rest of creation from the start to bring pleasure to God's heart. We are the crowning glory of His creation.

God loves us with perfect non-manipulative and unconditional love. He is on our side. He does not send the bad stuff – it is Satan that does that. He wants only the very best for us, and that best becomes ours if we will believe it and receive it.

God loves us absolutely, totally, infinitely – there is not a word to adequately describe His love for us. We do not need to ask for more of His love – what more could He do to show us how much He loves us, than by sacrificing His own Son for us. Jesus explained to His disciples –

> *"Greater love has no one than this, that someone lay down his life for his friends." (John 15:13)*

And Jesus put God's love into action, walking willingly into the physical, mental, emotional and spiritual agony of the Cross, so we could come into the intimate love relationship with His Father that He had always wanted restored, since the day Adam and Eve sinned. Jesus –

> *... for the joy that was set before him endured the cross, despising its shame. (Hebrews 12:2)*

The joy that Jesus could foresee as He went to the Cross was us coming into a love relationship with God. It could not happen under the law, because no-one could ever earn it or deserve it. But it was won for us through the Cross by grace, and we are called to receive it by faith. It was on the Cross that Jesus won forgiveness, salvation, healing and prosperity for us. It was all motivated by love.

God loves us so much and He wants us to start seeing ourselves the way He sees us, the way Jesus won for us to be, and to walk into the abundant life He came to give us.

Our love for God is a response to His love for us.

We love him, because he first loved us. (1 John 4:19)

He has done everything for us. We have a brand new perfect spirit – we are a new creation. We have God's authority to deal with sickness and demons, and God wants us to be His fellow-workers in it. All God's promises were fulfilled in Jesus and they can be fulfilled in our lives when we believe and receive. Choose to believe the truth of who you are in Jesus, and that all His promises apply to you, and you will find your love for Him will increase more and more.

And the more we love Him, the more we experience of His love. God has shown us and given us total unconditional love. We have it in total, but we do not experience it in total. We will never plumb its depth or scale its height or reach its width in this world, but God wants us to experience it more and more, going deeper and deeper into our relationship with Him. We do not need to ask God to give us more love; we need to ask Him to help us experience it more and more.

In our relationship with God, our love for Him grows as we put more and more confidence in Him and find Him always faithful and true. And that in turn increases our love for Him and we enter into that upward spiral of love and confidence. Gods' love for us is not increasing, it is already infinite, but our experience of it can increase. God is always showering us with love and drawing us with loving kindness, but we have a responsibility in this relationship too.

But you, beloved, keep building up yourselves on your most holy faith, praying in the Holy Spirit. [21]Keep yourselves in God's love. (Jude 1:20-21a)

Do not just sit back and wait to feel God's love for you. Start and continue to renew your mind so you can become transformed. Spend time in His Word and allow the Holy Spirit to bring it alive; spend time talking to Him and listening to HIm, thanking Him, worshiping Him, praising Him, speaking in tongues, telling Him you love Him, receiving His love. Meet together with your brothers and sisters in Jesus to learn more of God, to encourage each other, to worship together, to experience His presence among you, and just enjoy being family. Do not do it as a duty, do not make it a rule – just do it because you love Him, and because you know it is going to deepen your understanding and experience of Him and of His love for you. This will all help to build your faith and keep you in His love, and you will find your love for Him just keeps on growing.

God loves us totally and unconditionally. When we believe in His love and receive it, we not only start to love Him back, but our love for others also increases. It is as we know and experience more and more of God's love that our desire to reach out to others grows. We want to show them the love of God and bring healing and freedom into their lives. Jesus gave us just one commandment –

"A new commandment I give to you, that you love one another. Just as I have loved you, you also love one another. [35]By this everyone will know that you are my disciples, if you have love for one another."
(John 13:34-35)

Jesus was not saying that we earn our salvation by loving others; He was saying that the natural outcome of being saved is a heart of love for others. The Bible tells us that without love we are nothing and have nothing.

If I speak with the languages of men and of angels, but do not have love, I have become sounding brass, or a clanging cymbal. [2]If I have the gift of prophecy, and know all mysteries and all knowledge; and if I have all faith, so as to remove mountains, but do not have love, I am nothing. [3]If I give away all my goods to feed the poor, and if I give my body to be burnt, but do not have love, it profits me nothing. (1Corinthians 13:1-3)

It is essential that we show God's love to the people we minister to, and approach ministry with love at the centre. Experiencing the upward spiral of love and confidence with God motivates us to minister to people, and as we do so, we show them God's love and this draws them closer to God, so they can experience more of His love for themselves. As we love the people we minister to with the love of God, His love can speak into their mind and into their very heart.

As we minister to them, seeing them healed and delivered

and set free in the name of Jesus, and as we share God's truth with them, their confidence will grow in God and their love will then grow too and they will enter into that upward spiral of love and confidence in Him for themselves. And this completes the circle of God's love.

How can we not have confidence in such a God, such a Saviour, such a love. And how can we not help but want to draw others into it too, to be part of God's circle of love so they can experience the upward spiral of love and confidence with God for themselves.

All through this book I have sought to help you to have confidence in God, in Jesus, in the power and in yourself as a child of God, so you can step out and minister in confidence. But I encourage you to make everything I have said your own truth. I call it making it your own revelation.

Do not wait for God to make you believe it – He will not. He will never compromise your free will. But as you study His Word and meditate on it, the Holy Spirit will reveal its truth to you personally – to your mind and to your heart, so you can know it and experience it more and more. He will encourage you to believe and draw you deeper and deeper into God's love for you.

And when God's truth is rooted and established in you, you can then minister it to others in complete confidence, leading them into healing and freedom and wholeness and into who they are in Jesus – the people God designed them to be.

Keep yourself in God's love and allow His love to flow out of you to others. Do not focus on yourself – focus on God in whom you can have complete confidence. Focus on Jesus who sacrificed everything for you, so you could walk in freedom, health and wholeness. Focus on the Holy Spirit who is in you and has filled you with God's power.

Remember you have the power that raised Jesus from the dead living in you. You may not feel it, but it is true – believe what God's Word tells you, not your feelings. Refuse to believe any negative thoughts about yourself – you are a child of God and as such are more than a conqueror.

You have the Holy Spirit, you have the Word of God, you have the name of Jesus – you can minister to others in complete confidence. Make that important decision once and for all to believe what God's Word says, regardless of what you see, feel or experience, or what other people say, whoever they are. Follow Jesus and minister to others – just get on and do it, and praise God as you start to see signs and wonders before your eyes.

As I bring this book to a close, hear Jesus speaking personally to you once more as you read these adapted sayings of Jesus out loud to yourself.

"In me you may have peace. In the world you have trouble; but cheer up! I have overcome the world." *(John 16:33b)*

"I came that you may have life, and may have it abundantly." *(John 10:10b)*

"Most certainly I tell you, you who believe in me, the works that I did on earth, you will do also; and you will do greater works than these, because I have gone to my Father." *(John 14:12)*

"For most certainly I tell you, when you tell this mountain, 'Be taken up and cast into the sea,' and do not doubt in your heart, but believe that what you say is happening; you shall have whatever you say." *(Mark 11:23)*

"These signs will accompany you: in my name you will cast out demons; you will speak with new languages; [18]you will take up serpents; and if you drink any deadly thing, it will in no way hurt you; you will lay hands on the sick, and they will recover." *(Mark 16:17-18)*

"Heal the sick and cast out demons. Freely you received, so freely give." *(Matthew 10:8)*

"I am with you always, even to the end of the age." *(Matthew 28:20b)*

Now confirm yourself in the love of God and praise Him –

For I am persuaded that neither death, nor life, nor angels, nor principalities, nor things present, nor things to come, nor powers, [39]nor height, nor depth, nor any other created thing will be able to separate me from God's love which is in Christ Jesus my Lord. *(Romans 8:38-39)*

Now thanks be to God, who always leads me in triumph in Christ, and reveals through me the sweet aroma of his knowledge in every place. *(2 Corinthians 2:14)*

Bible Verses

The Word of God is absolute truth and power. Below are some Bible verses arranged under subject headings in alphabetical order. Use them to strengthen and sustain your confidence in God and in Jesus, and also to give away to the people you minister to.

1. DELIVERANCE

"He has sent me to heal the broken hearted, to proclaim release to the captives, recovering of sight to the blind, to deliver those who are crushed." (Luke 4:18b)

But thanks be to God, who gives us the victory through our Lord Jesus Christ. (1 Corinthians 15:57)

... the weapons of our warfare are not of the flesh, but mighty before God to the throwing down of strongholds. (2 Corinthians 10:4)

Stand firm therefore in the liberty by which Christ has made us free, and do not be entangled again with a yoke of bondage. (Galatians 5:1)

To this end the Son of God was revealed: that he might destroy the works of the devil. (1 John 3:8b)

2. ENCOURAGEMENT

"For I know the thoughts that I think towards you," says the LORD, "thoughts of peace, and not of evil, to give you hope and a future." (Jeremiah 29:11)

"Behold, I am with you always, even to the end of the age." (Matthew 28:20b)

"The thief only comes to steal, kill, and destroy. I came that they may have life, and may have it abundantly." (John 10:10)

For you are not under law, but under grace. (Romans 6:14b)

There is therefore now no condemnation to those who are in Christ Jesus. (Romans 8:1a)

We know that all things work together for good for those who love God, for those who are called according to his purpose. (Romans 8:28)

Do not be conformed to this world, but be transformed by the renewing of your mind, so that you may prove what is the good, well-pleasing, and perfect will of God. (Romans 12:2)

For however many are the promises of God, in him is the "Yes." Therefore also through him is the "Amen", to the glory of God through us. (2 Corinthians 1:20)

For we are God's fellow workers. (1 Corinthians 3:9a)

(Continued overleaf)

Blessed be the God and Father of our Lord Jesus Christ, who has blessed us with every spiritual blessing in the heavenly places in Christ. (Ephesians 1:3)

*But we all, with unveiled face seeing the glory of the Lord as in a mirror, are transformed into the same image from glory to glory, even as from the Lord, the Spirit.
(2 Corinthians 3:18)*

Therefore if anyone is in Christ, he is a new creation. The old things have passed away. Behold, all things have become new. (2 Corinthians 5:17)

(God) ... raised us up with him, and made us to sit with him in the heavenly places in Christ Jesus. (Ephesians 2:6)

3. FAITH

"For most certainly I tell you, if you have faith as a grain of mustard seed, you will tell this mountain, 'Move from here to there,' and it will move; and nothing will be impossible for you." (Matthew 17:20b)

Jesus answered them, "Have faith in God. ^{23}For most certainly I tell you, whoever may tell this mountain, 'Be taken up and cast into the sea,' and doesn't doubt in his heart, but believes that what he says is happening; he shall have whatever he says." (Mark 11:22-23)

"Therefore I tell you, all things whatever you pray and ask for, believe that you have received them, and you shall have them." (Mark 11:24)

"Your faith has made you well. Go in peace." (Luke 8:48b)

"By faith in his name, his name has made this man strong, whom you see and know. Yes, the faith which is through him has given him this perfect soundness in the presence of you all." (Acts 3:16)

So faith comes by hearing, and hearing by the word of God. (Romans 10:17)

... by grace you have been saved through faith, and that not of yourselves; it is the gift of God. (Ephesians 2:8)

4. FORGIVENESS

The goodness of God leads you to repentance.
(Romans 2:4b)

Much more then, being now justified by his blood, we will be saved from God's wrath through him. (Romans 5:9)

There is therefore now no condemnation to those who are in Christ Jesus. (Romans 8:1a)

... God was in Christ reconciling the world to himself, not reckoning to them their trespasses, and having committed to us the word of reconciliation. (2 Corinthians 5:19)

You were dead through your trespasses and the uncircumcision of your flesh. He made you alive together with him, having forgiven us all our trespasses.
(Colossians 2:13)

... bearing with one another, and forgiving each other, if any man has a complaint against any; even as Christ forgave you, so you also do. (Colossians 3:13)

"I will remember their sins and lawless deeds no more."
(Hebrews 8:12b)

And he is the atoning sacrifice for our sins, and not for ours only, but also for the whole world. (1 John 2:2)

5. GOD'S WORD

He sends his word, and heals them, and delivers them from their graves. (Psalm 107:20)

*My son, attend to my words. Turn your ear to my sayings.
[21]Let them not depart from your eyes. Keep them in the centre of your heart. [22]For they are life to those who find them, and health to their whole body. (Proverbs 4:20-22)*

"... so is my word that goes out of my mouth: it will not return to me void, but it will accomplish that which I please, and it will prosper in the thing I sent it to do." (Isaiah 55:11)

*"If you remain in my word, then you are truly my disciples.
[32]You will know the truth, and the truth will make you free."
(John 8:31b-32)*

*.. take ... the sword of the Spirit, which is the word of God.
(Ephesians 6:17b)*

*... the word of God, which also works in you who believe.
(1 Thessalonians 2:13b)*

*Every Scripture is God-breathed and profitable for teaching, for reproof, for correction, and for instruction in righteousness, [17]that each person who belongs to God may be complete, thoroughly equipped for every good work.
(2 Timothy 3:16-17)*

6. HEALING – EMOTIONAL

He sends his word, and heals them, and delivers them from their graves. (Psalm 107:20)

He heals the broken in heart, and binds up their wounds. (Psalm 147:3)

"He has sent me to heal the broken hearted, to proclaim release to the captives, recovering of sight to the blind, to deliver those who are crushed." (Luke 4:18b)

Do not be conformed to this world, but be transformed by the renewing of your mind, so that you may prove what is the good, well-pleasing, and perfect will of God. (Romans 12:2)

7. HEALING – PHYSICAL

Praise the LORD, my soul, and do not forget all his benefits;
³who forgives all your sins; who heals all your diseases.
(Psalm 103:2-3)

He took our infirmities, and bore our diseases.
(Matthew 8:17b)

"Again, assuredly I tell you, that if two of you will agree on
earth concerning anything that they will ask, it will be done
for them by my Father who is in heaven." (Matthew 18:19)

"He has sent me to heal the broken hearted, to proclaim
release to the captives, recovering of sight to the blind, to
deliver those who are crushed." (Luke 4:18b)

"Your faith has made you well. Go in peace." (Luke 8:48b)

"By faith in his name, his name has made this man strong,
whom you see and know. Yes, the faith which is through him
has given him this perfect soundness in the presence of you
all." (Acts 3:16)

You were healed by his wounds. (1 Peter 2:24b)

8. THE HOLY SPIRIT

"If you then, being evil, know how to give good gifts to your children, how much more will your heavenly Father give the Holy Spirit to those who ask him?" (Luke 11:13)

"But the Counsellor, the Holy Spirit, whom the Father will send in my name, he will teach you all things, and will remind you of all that I said to you." (John 14:26)

"However when he, the Spirit of truth, has come, he will guide you into all truth." (John 16:13a)

"... you will receive power when the Holy Spirit has come upon you." (Acts 1:8a)

... the Spirit also helps our weaknesses, for we do not know how to pray as we ought. But the Spirit himself makes intercession for us with groanings which cannot be uttered. (Romans 8:26)

Or do not you know that your body is a temple of the Holy Spirit who is in you, whom you have from God? (1 Corinthians 6:19)

Now he who establishes us with you in Christ, and anointed us, is God; ^{22}who also sealed us, and gave us the down payment of the Spirit in our hearts. (2 Corinthians 1:21-22)

But the fruit of the Spirit is love, joy, peace, patience, kindness, goodness, faith, ^{23}gentleness, and self-control. (Galatians 5:22-23a)

... be filled with the Spirit, [19]speaking to one another in psalms, hymns, and spiritual songs; singing, and making melody in your heart to the Lord. (Ephesians 5:18b-19)

9. LOVE

"Yes, I have loved you with an everlasting love. Therefore I have drawn you with loving kindness." (Jeremiah 31:3b)

"A new commandment I give to you, that you love one another. Just as I have loved you, you also love one another." (John 13:34)

For God so loved the world, that he gave his one and only Son, that whoever believes in him should not perish, but have eternal life. (John 3:16)

In this is love, not that we loved God, but that he loved us, and sent his Son as the atoning sacrifice for our sins. (1 John 4:10)

God commends his own love towards us, in that while we were yet sinners, Christ died for us. (Romans 5:8)

See how great a love the Father has given to us, that we should be called children of God! (1 John 3:1a)

God's love has been poured into our hearts through the Holy Spirit who was given to us. (Romans 5:5b)

For I am persuaded that neither death, nor life, nor angels, nor principalities, nor things present, nor things to come, nor powers, [39] nor height, nor depth, nor any other created thing will be able to separate (me) *us from God's love which is in Christ Jesus our Lord. (Romans 8:38-39)*

10. PROTECTION

No weapon that is formed against you will prevail; and you will condemn every tongue that rises against you in judgement. (Isaiah 54:17a)

The weapons of our warfare are not of the flesh, but mighty before God to the throwing down of strongholds, [5]throwing down imaginations and every high thing that is exalted against the knowledge of God, and bringing every thought into captivity to the obedience of Christ.
(2 Corinthians 10:4-5)

Therefore put on the whole armour of God, that you may be able to withstand in the evil day, and, having done all, to stand. (Ephesians 6:13)

Stand therefore, having the utility belt of truth buckled around your waist and having put on the breastplate of righteousness, [15]and having fitted your feet with the preparation of the Good News of peace; [16]above all, taking up the shield of faith, with which you will be able to quench all the fiery darts of the evil one. [17]And take the helmet of salvation and the sword of the Spirit, which is the Word of God. (Ephesians 6:14-17)

But the Lord is faithful, who will establish you, and guard you from the evil one. (2 Thessalonians 3:3)

Be subject therefore to God. Resist the devil, and he will flee from you. (James 4:7)

(Continued overleaf)

Greater is he who is in you than he who is in the world. (1 John 4:4b)

If God is for us, who can be against us? (Romans 8:31a)

Don't you be afraid, for I am with you. Don't be dismayed, for I am your God. I will strengthen you. Yes, I will help you. Yes, I will uphold you with the right hand of my righteousness. (Isaiah 41:10)

11. PROVISION

"Give, and it will be given to you: good measure, pressed down, shaken together, and running over, will be given to you. For with the same measure you measure it will be measured back to you." (Luke 6:38)

"Therefore I tell you, all things whatever you pray and ask for, believe that you have received them, and you shall have them." (Mark 11:24)

"Your Father knows that you need these things." (Luke 12:30b)

For you know the grace of our Lord Jesus Christ, that, though he was rich, yet for your sakes he became poor, that you through his poverty might become rich. (2 Corinthians 8:9)

My God will supply every need of yours according to his riches in glory in Christ Jesus. (Philippians 4:19)

12. SALVATION

For God so loved the world, that he gave his one and only Son, that whoever believes in him should not perish, but have eternal life. (John 3:16)

For God didn't send his Son into the world to judge the world, but that the world should be saved through him. (John 3:17)

"I am the way, the truth, and the life. No one comes to the Father, except through me." (John 14:6)

Being therefore justified by faith, we have peace with God through our Lord Jesus Christ. (Romans 5:1)

If you will confess with your mouth that Jesus is Lord, and believe in your heart that God raised him from the dead, you will be saved. (Romans 10:9)

For God didn't appoint us to wrath, but to the obtaining of salvation through our Lord Jesus Christ.
(1 Thessalonians 5:9)

13. THE VICTORY OF THE CROSS

To this end the Son of God was revealed: that he might destroy the works of the devil. (1 John 3:8b)

You were dead through your trespasses and the uncircumcision of your flesh. He made you alive together with him, having forgiven us all our trespasses, [14]wiping out the handwriting in ordinances which was against us. He has taken it out of the way, nailing it to the cross. [15]Having stripped the principalities and the powers, he made a show of them openly, triumphing over them in it.
(Colossians 2:13-15)

Since then the children have shared in flesh and blood, he also himself in the same way partook of the same, that through death he might bring to nothing him who had the power of death, that is, the devil, [15]and might deliver all of them who through fear of death were all their lifetime subject to bondage. (Hebrews 2:14-15)

But God, being rich in mercy, for his great love with which he loved us, [5]even when we were dead through our trespasses, made us alive together with Christ—by grace you have been saved— [6]and raised us up with him, and made us to sit with him in the heavenly places in Christ Jesus. (Ephesians 2:4-6)

I have been crucified with Christ, and it is no longer I that live, but Christ lives in me. That life which I now live in the flesh, I live by faith in the Son of God, who loved me, and gave himself up for me. (Galatians 2:20)

(Continued overleaf)

He himself bore our sins in his body on the tree, that we, having died to sins, might live to righteousness. You were healed by his wounds. (1 Peter 2:24)

Christ redeemed us from the curse of the law, having become a curse for us. (Galatians 3:13a)

For you know the grace of our Lord Jesus Christ, that, though he was rich, yet for your sakes he became poor, that you through his poverty might become rich. (2 Corinthians 8:9)

He did this once for all, when he offered up himself. (Hebrews 7:27b)

Much more then, being now justified by his blood, we will be saved from God's wrath through him. [10]For if while we were enemies, we were reconciled to God through the death of his Son, much more, being reconciled, we will be saved by his life. (Romans 5:9-10)

"If therefore the Son makes you free, you will be free indeed." (John 8:36)

Thanks be to God, who gives us the victory through our Lord Jesus Christ. (1 Corinthians 15:57)

14. WISDOM

Trust in the LORD with all your heart, and do not lean on your own understanding. (Proverbs 3:5)

The foolishness of God is wiser than men, and the weakness of God is stronger than men. (1 Corinthians 1:25)

Because of him, you are in Christ Jesus, who was made to us wisdom from God. (1 Corinthians 1:30a)

... that they may know the mystery of God, both of the Father and of Christ, [3]in whom all the treasures of wisdom and knowledge are hidden. (Colossians 2:2b-3)

But if any of you lacks wisdom, let him ask of God, who gives to all liberally and without reproach; and it will be given to him. [6]But let him ask in faith, without any doubting, for he who doubts is like a wave of the sea, driven by the wind and tossed. (James 1:5-6)

But the wisdom that is from above is first pure, then peaceful, gentle, reasonable, full of mercy and good fruits, without partiality, and without hypocrisy. (James 3:17)

Understanding Christianity

Katherine Hilditch has written a series of booklets
to help Christians and non-Christians
understand more about God's love
and all He has done for them through Jesus.

They are available to read online
or download and print out
free of charge at

www.understandingchristianity.co.uk

There is no limit to the number of copies
you can print out from the website
for your own use or to give away

Printed in Great Britain
by Amazon